CONSCIOUS UNION
WITH GOD

Other Writings of Joel S. Goldsmith

CONSCIOUS UNION
WITH GOD

Joel S. Goldsmith

Edited By
Lorraine Sinkler

I-Level
Acropolis Books, Publisher
Atlanta, Georgia

Conscious Union With God
First Acropolis Books Edition 2000
© 1962, 1990 by Joel Goldsmith

Second Printing, 2004

All Bible quotations are taken from THE KING JAMES VERSION

Published by Acropolis Books, Inc. Publisher, under an arrangement with Citadel Press, an imprint of Carol Publishing Group.

Printed in the United States of America

For information contact:

Acropolis Books, Inc.
Atlanta, Georgia

http://www.acropolisbooks.com

Cover Design by Tonya Beach Creative Services

Library of Congress Cataloging-in-Publication Data

Goldsmith, Joel S., 1892–1964.
    Conscious union with God / Joel S. Goldsmith; edited by Lorraine Sinkler.
- - 1ˢᵗ Acropolis books ed.
        p.   cm.
Originally published: Secaucus, N.J. : University Books, 1962.
Includes bibliographical references.
ISBN 1-889051-48-9 (hardcover : alk. paper)
ISBN 1-889051-49-7 (paperback : alk. paper)
    1. New Thought.   I. Sinkler, Lorraine.   II. Title.
BF639.G5577 2000
299'.93--dc21   00-022093
                                                                         CIP

This book is printed on acid free paper that meets the American National
Standards Institute Z 39.48 Standard

Holy Spirit of God, the Spirit of Truth, help me to discern in this book the Truth that comes from God, from that which does not come from God (i.e. a merely human construct, and not divine)

Except the Lord build the house,
they labour in vain that build it. . . .

—Psalm 127

Help me to discern the best (God's Truth) and leave the rest. I rely on the Spirit of God's Truth to guide me accordingly.

"Illumination dissolves all material ties and binds men together with the golden chains of spiritual understanding; it acknowledges only the leadership of the Christ; it has no ritual or rule but the divine, (impersonal) universal Love; no other worship than the inner Flame that is ever lit at the shrine of Spirit. This union is the free state of spiritual brotherhood. The only restraint is the discipline of Soul; therefore, we know liberty without license; we are a united universe without physical limits, a divine service to God without ceremony or creed. The illumined walk without fear—by Grace."

?

— *The Infinite Way* by Joel S. Goldsmith

God loves me personally. He calls me by name.

TABLE OF CONTENTS

Table of Contents

TABLE OF CONTENTS

Consciousness Union with God

INTRODUCTION

Preaching without practice is one of the deadliest of sins. For example, the scriptural passage, so fundamental to all spiritual teaching, "Except the Lord build the house, they labour in vain that build it,"[1] is a beautiful quotation, but it remains only a preachment until, and unless, it is understood and practiced.

If I were to attempt to teach truth humanly through books, classes, or recorded messages, it would result only in failure. Moreover, if you think that there is some new truth to be learned humanly, you will be disappointed because there is not a single new truth in the entire world. The truth revealed in this book is not my truth or my message, but the word of God which has been imparting itself to universal consciousness throughout all time. That word of God is already embodied in your consciousness, and this truth, which is already your consciousness, is now being unveiled to you within you.

Unless God is my consciousness, there will be no truth expressing itself through, or as, me; and, moreover, unless God is your consciousness, you will not understand the truth that is being presented. But, since God is universal consciousness and since God is my consciousness, truth is expressing itself as this book—God expressing and revealing Itself.*

---

* In the spiritual literature of the world, the varying concepts of God are indicated by the use of such words as "Father," "Mother," "Soul," "Spirit," "Principle," "Love," and "Life." Therefore, in this book the author has used the pronouns "He" and "It," or "Himself" and "Itself," interchangeably in referring to God.

Furthermore, since God is your consciousness, God will be revealing Itself unto Itself. Consciousness will be expressing Its truth unto Itself. Truth will not pass from me to you, and it will not pass from God to you: The entire activity of truth will take place in the one Consciousness, the consciousness of me which is the consciousness of you.

The purpose of this book is to bring to light the truth of being, but no one can put it into practice for you but you, yourself, and the progress you make will depend upon what you absorb of that which is unfolded and revealed in these pages. Therefore, in some measure, you must begin to use what is given, chapter by chapter, in order to assimilate the more advanced lessons.

This is no different from taking piano lessons or any other kind of lessons. You go to your teacher and take a lesson, but if you do not practice, you will receive no benefit from another lesson the next day. In the same way, your unfoldment, understanding, and progress in truth will be in the degree of your putting each and every one of these lessons into practice.

This message has nothing whatsoever to do with a human person called a teacher, but only with a teaching or revelation. Its main purpose is not the healing of physical bodies, nor is it the adding of ten or a hundred dollars a week to anyone's income. The Infinite Way is not primarily concerned with temporal or human improvements: It is concerned with the mission of the Christ, which is to set you free, to set you free *spiritually*–free from your belief in bondage to person, place, thing, circumstance, or condition.

~ 1 ~

THE BASIS OF SPIRITUAL HEALING

Spiritual healing is brought about through the realization of the Christ in individual consciousness. God, the individual Consciousness of this universe, is the one and only consciousness. However, since God is the consciousness of me and God is the consciousness of you, and because there is only this one consciousness, truth becomes effective in the consciousness of anyone who tunes in to it. Therefore, any truth that reveals itself within our consciousness instantaneously reveals itself to the person appearing as our patient.

Sometimes, people who are not associated with us in any way, either as friends, relatives, students, or patients—someone in a hospital or a prison, someone on a desert island, someone who is reaching out for help to his highest concept of God—may be healed even though they do not know us and we do not know them; or even if they do know us, they may not know that we are on this path, and, therefore, would not know why they were healed.

There is only one Life, one Consciousness, one Soul; but that One is the consciousness of you and the consciousness of me. That is why we do not have to try to reach anyone. When we are in this conscious oneness, we become so much a part of one another that what one is thinking about Truth, or God, the other is hearing, but no transference of thought is involved and should not be so construed. We are not one in our humanhood: We are one in the Christ, and all that is being imparted is the divine idea flowing in consciousness.

For that reason, those who are aware of the principle of one power need never be concerned about suffering from other people's thoughts. All the suffering on earth, regardless of its form or nature, is a product of the universal belief in two powers; and therefore, universal harmony will only be restored when God is revealed as Omnipotence. There is only one mind and that mind is the instrument of the one Spirit, or God. Human thinking, which is the product of a mind unaware of its proper function as an instrument of God, never rises higher than the person in whose mind it is taking place.

For example, if someone were sitting here repeating, "Two times two is five," our own mathematical sense would be a protection to us, and we would not accept that incorrect statement. He might say, "You are dead!" but our own sense of life would be a protection, and we would not be troubled by such erroneous thinking.

In some forms of mental practice, experiments have been conducted which prove that an individual cannot be induced to do anything which violates his own integrity unless it is by his own conscious choice. No amount of human thinking consciously directed at a person can ever make anyone violate his own integrity; and therefore, when anyone does wrong, it is because he himself is consciously violating his own sense of right. It all lies within one's own being.

Spiritual Freedom

The disciples understood little of Jesus' mission. In the three years that they were with Jesus, although they had almost daily contact with him and with his thought and work, there were few who gave evidence of being deeply touched by his message. He was not able to bring about much spirituality in Judas, and he did not have too great success with Peter, and even less with most of the other disciples. John, of course, caught the full and complete message.

The coming of the Messiah had been prophesied for centuries, but the Hebrews had no concept of the Messiah as a teaching or as a divine idea. They thought that the Messiah, when he came, would be a man who would lead them into freedom. Freedom from what? Freedom from bondage to Caesar, from being slaves of Caesar; freedom, probably, from some of the practices imposed by their religion, because the people of Jesus' day were looking for a physical freedom, a temporal freedom, and probably they thought that the Messiah might come as a king to give them that freedom. In this they were disappointed. They did not understand that Jesus' mission was not of this world.

Jesus came with the divine idea of spiritual freedom. He hoped that by setting the people of his day free in their consciousness—free from slavery to person and thing—they would be free in fact. But the Hebrews were looking for a human emancipator who would free them from intolerable conditions, and they failed to understand the mission of the Christ. For that reason only a few of them caught the vision and benefitted by it.

Today, let no one make the same mistake about the mission of the Infinite Way. Its purpose is the unfoldment and revelation of spiritual being, the harmonious and eternal manifestation of God, Good. It does not attempt to change, correct, or reform any person. Therefore, our work lies within our own being and consists of reaching that spiritual consciousness in which there is no temptation to accept the universe and individual being as other than God appearing as the universe and as individual being.

In the commonly accepted sense of metaphysical healing practice, health is usually sought as the opposite or absence of disease, goodness and morality as the opposite or absence of badness and immorality; but in this unfoldment, we do not attempt to heal the body, remove disease, or reform sinners. We do not seek health in what Jesus called "this world" because *"My kingdom* is not of this world,"[1] that is, the Christ-work is not in the realm of human concepts. We understand health to be the quality and activity of Soul, always expressed as perfect and immortal body. Even a harmonious human body does not necessarily express health because health is more than the absence of disease: It is an eternal state of spiritual being. Furthermore, human goodness is but the opposite of human badness and is not the spiritual state of being which we must realize and achieve in our approach to life.

Although this message does not concern itself with human health or disease, material wealth or poverty, personal goodness or badness, nevertheless, the attainment of the consciousness of God appearing as individual being results in what appears to human sense as health, wealth, and goodness. These, however, represent the finite concepts of that spiritual harmony which actually is always present.

When we are no longer in bondage to the belief that we are slaves to some person or circumstance and when we are no longer slaves to dollar bills, we shall be truly free forever. Then it will make no difference to us what kind of a political or economic system exists in our world. We shall be abundantly provided with whatever form of supply is necessary under the particular form of government under which we are living. And if we were in prison, we would still be free. We would be like those people of old who said, "Imprison me, you cannot! My body, you can put in jail—but not me!"

Mind, or consciousness, cannot be confined to a room or to a chair. The mind can wander around at will and can be trained so to rise above corporeal sense as actually to be out in this world with the sense of being free of the body, although we do not leave the body. It is not possible to leave our body because our body and we are one, but we can leave the corporeal sense of it and be so free spiritually that we are confined neither to time nor space. That is what happens when we gain our spiritual freedom.

In that spiritual freedom, we surmount all sense of limitation. For example, we do not stop using dollars, but we do not worry about them. The dollars will come, and even though we continue to use them, we shall no longer be limited or confined by the concept that dollars constitute supply.

As long as we think of money as supply, we will not demonstrate spiritual freedom as related to supply. Even if our income should be doubled, we should not congratulate ourselves on having made a demonstration, if we still believe that money is supply! Money is not supply. *I am supply: Consciousness is supply.* This indefinable Essence, called Spirit, which we are, is supply, and that is omnipresent, omnipotent, and omniscient.

Understanding the Nature of God

Our entire spiritual life depends upon our ability to know God, and unless we understand the omnipresence and omnipotence of God, we shall make no progress in this work.

Throughout the ages, many names have been given to God: Abraham knew God as Friend. In the ancient Hindu Scriptures, dating back thousands of years and comprising some of the earliest literature given to the world on the subject of God, God is referred to as "Mother" and sometimes as "Father." The great modern Hindu mystic, Ramakrishna, knew God as Mother Kali; but often terms, such as "Mind," "Principle," "Soul," "Light," "Spirit," "Love," and other of the well-known synonyms for God, will also be found in the Hindu Scriptures. Yet because it was the nature of the primitive Hindus, as of the primitive Hebrews, to personalize, they brought God closer to themselves in the way which they understood best–as a loving Mother and occasionally as Father.

In the nineteenth century, Sanskrit scholars translated many of the great Hindu classics into the German and English languages so that, for the first time, the West had the opportunity of becoming familiar with Hindu terminology. The result was that many of its concepts for God seeped into the literature of the nineteenth century. The term "Father-Mother" as a synonym for God gained widespread acceptance through its incorporation into the teaching of Christian Science by Mary Baker Eddy. Through her use of this term in Christian Science literature, it later was incorporated in many other metaphysical teachings. And so God has been known as Mother, sometimes as Father, and also as Father-Mother. None of these terms was meant to indicate gender or to mean that God was either male or female. Rather, such endearing terms connote the tender, loving, and protective qualities of a mother, and the stern, law-giving, protective, sustaining, and maintaining qualities of a father.

So, when God comes to your individual consciousness, He comes in such a tender way that you may still use the term, Father or Mother. More and more people, however, are beginning to think of God as Light and Life; and, when God is realized in individual consciousness as Life or as Light, there is no sense of male or female, just a sense of God as the universal life which permeates all form. God is the life which permeates your form–the life permeating the form of the tree, of the animal, and of the flower, impersonal, but nonetheless life.

God is Spirit, and Spirit is the substance and the essence of which all things are formed–all that is in the earth and sky, air and water. Spiritual creation is formed of this indestructible and indivisible Substance, or Spirit, called God.

Spiritual Consciousness Reveals Reality

You may wonder then, why there are such things as rotting trees or erupting volcanoes. Are they, also, of the essence of God? No, they represent our concept of that which actually is there. In the kingdom of God, there is never a rotting tree, nor are there any destructive or disruptive forces operative. The German mystic, Jacob Boehme, saw through the trees and through the grass to reality. To all mystics, it is as though the world opens up and they see the world as God made it.

God is the underlying substance and reality of all form, but what we see, hear, taste, touch, or smell is the product of the human mind, of mortal, material, finite sense. The sum total of human beings in the world, under what is termed material law—medical, theological, or economic—has set up this finite sense of the universe which they see, hear, taste, touch, or smell.

Nothing is what it appears to be. All of us could look at the same object, and every one of us might see it differently. Why? Because each one of us interprets it in the light of the education, environment, and background of his individual experience. To understand that what we see represents only our concept of that which is actually there is important, because on this point we make or lose our healing consciousness. God created all that was created and all that He created is good. Therefore, this whole world, whether seen as human beings, animals, or plants, is God manifest. But when we see it, we do not see it as it is: We see only our finite concept of it.

This is vitally important because it is on this premise that all spiritual healing is based, and a lack of recognition of this point accounts for ninety-five percent of the failure in spiritual healing. Many metaphysicians are trying to heal the physical body, and it cannot be healed, because there is nothing a metaphysician can do to a physical body, but when he changes his concept of the body, the body responds to that higher concept. Then the patient says, "I have been healed!" He has not been healed: He was perfect in the beginning. What was wrong was not in the body, but in his false concept of himself and of his body.*

If you can grasp this idea, it may save you from making the fatal mistake of trying to heal somebody or

---

* For a more complete explanation of this point, see the chapter on "The True Sense of the Universe" in the author's *Spiritual Interpretation of Scripture,* © 1947 Joel S. Goldsmith (Marina del Ray, CA, DeVorss & Company)

somebody's body. When I see your body through spiritual sense, I behold you as God made you, and you will declare that you have been healed. God's creation is intact; it is perfect and harmonious, and that perfect and harmonious creation is right here and now. But this cannot be seen with the physical eyes. It can be discerned only through spiritual vision, spiritual sense—through spiritual consciousness, or what is called Christ-consciousness.

Do not try to reform the outer picture. When you meet with thievery, drunkenness, or any form of degradation, do not look at it, but through it. Do not look with the eyes. Close the eyes or at least turn away. Look through the individual, beholding through your spiritual sense the reality of his being, and you will bring about what the world calls healing. With your inner, God-given, spiritual sense, look into the heart of every man and see the Christ, and there you will find the most wonderful healing force there is in the world. Then let your feeling guide you. Get a sense, or a feeling, of the Christ sitting right there in the center of individual being, and when you reach that Christ you will have an instantaneous healing.

To bring about a healing of sin or disease, do not be concerned about a human being or body. Become silent within your being: Feel the presence of God, the presence of Good, the divine or inner Sense, and then you will not be tempted to think of any one person. It is not necessary to think of the name of the person turning to you for help, of his form, or of his disease. The all-knowing Intelligence knows, and therefore when you feel a sense of Soul which takes him in, you will have witnessed a healing.

Conducting a Healing Practice

In conducting your healing practice, be careful that you do not smugly repeat statements of truth to your patients, that you do not give them beautiful quotations from Scripture or metaphysical writings, unless you yourself have had some measure of consciousness of that truth. Remember, it is far better to say nothing to your patients other than a "Leave this with me," or an "I will help you," or "I will be with you," or "Call me again in the morning"—far better to give them no statement of truth, but merely your assurance that you, with your realization of the presence of God, are consciously with them in prayer and realization.

When your consciousness is imbued with the spirit of truth—not merely the letter of truth, but the spirit of truth—healing will take place. Then you can explain to your patients what the truth is, giving them statements of truth which you have proved or demonstrated, and which have become a part of your consciousness. They will then not only be glad to hear these statements, but will feel their truth. Giving your patients or students quotations and statements of truth of which you yourself do not have the consciousness is like giving them a stone when they ask for bread. Rather give them a simple statement, one which you have demonstrated over and over again, and which, therefore, you know to be true. Unless you can do that, give them the healing silence. Say nothing, but feel within your being this healing Christ.

Remember this: You are not called upon to heal a person; you are not called upon to remove some terrible disease; you are not called upon to change the activity of a human body. All that you are ever called upon to do is to realize the spiritual nature of the omnipresent God and God's perfect creation. You are called upon to feel a living Presence, to feel this living Presence at the center of your being.

In every case to which you are called, the real call is for your realization of God as the life of man, God as the mind and the Soul and the law and the substance and the cause. Stating these things, however, does not constitute spiritual healing. It is feeling them; it is an actual spiritual awareness within your own being.

Do not try to reach your patient. Do not try to get your thought across to a patient. Only be sure that within your own being you feel the truth, you feel the rightness, you feel the spiritual sense of being. Then your patient will respond. Do not take your patient into your thought—do not take his name or the nature of his disease or what he looks like—and above all, never think that you must convey or transfer some thought to your patient.

It makes no difference what the claim or problem is. When the Christ of you touches the Christ of your patient, there is healing. Do not try to heal anybody humanly, either mentally or physically. Try to be silent in the center of your being and feel the Christ, knowing that all this is taking place in the one Heart, the heart of God, which is the heart of you. You must feel a conscious oneness with God. God is all-inclusive and since God is all-inclusive, you and I must be included in that God-being, so that when I am at-one with God, I am at-one with you; and when you are at-one with God, you are at-one with me. *My conscious oneness with God constitutes my oneness with you and with every spiritual being and with every activity of God that is included in my life.* All of these are divine ideas, the form of which we translate in terms of our human needs.

Just as your body is a spiritual body in God, neither male nor female, so when you are touching the Christ at the center of your being, which is the Christ of every individual, there is only pure love, pure Spirit. Because of human sense, however, the qualities of God are interpreted as both male and female.

In the same way, the idea of transportation can be translated into a donkey, an airplane, a streetcar, or an automobile. These represent only the human concepts of the divine idea of transportation. The truth about transportation is found in one word, instantaneity: *I* * am everywhere—here, there, and everywhere! That is the truth about spiritual transportation. That is why it is just as easy for a practitioner in San Francisco to heal someone in China as to heal someone who is physically present with him.

Awareness of God Is Necessary

In *The Infinite Way,* there is a chapter on "Meditation,"[2] which outlines a course in what may be called spiritual preparation. The first part of this preparation is the practice of awakening in the morning in the conscious realization of your oneness with God. "Except the Lord build the house, they labour in vain that build it."[3] If you do not consciously bring God into your experience with your first waking moment, you may have lost the opportunity of having God with you on every occasion throughout the day.

---

*The word "I," italicized, refers to God.

Perhaps as you read this, you may think, "Oh, God is omnipresent; God is always with me!" Do not believe that, because it is not true at all! That is one of those clichés—one of those quotations!

It is true that God is omnipresent. It is true that God is right where you are. But if it is true that God is omnipresent, then God must have been present when all our boys were killed at the front or when of old the Christians were thrown to the lions, or when in the last few decades thousands of innocent people were slaughtered in concentration camps. What was God doing while all these horrors were going on? Was He there? Then, why was He not helping? Certainly, God was there, but God is not a person and God cannot look down on you and tell you He is sorry for the suffering you are enduring. God is omnipresent in the hospitals, in the prisons, at the battle front. God is omnipresent! But of what good is that to anybody? Of what good is it to you? Only this: In proportion to your conscious awareness of the presence of God is God available in every instance.

God is present! Certainly. Electricity was present throughout the ages even when people were using whale oil and kerosene oil. But of what benefit was electricity to them? None, because there was no conscious realization of the presence of electricity.

Jesus could have been traveling around the Holy Land in an airplane, too. And what about the Hebrews on their long trek across the sands? It takes forty minutes today! Think! That which took forty years then takes only forty minutes today. The laws of aero-dynamics were present and available to them, but there was no conscious awareness of them, although these laws could have been implemented had there been any knowledge of them.

Electricity is present today as it always has been, but now, because of a conscious awareness of its laws, it gives us light, heat, and power. God is present here and now, but there must be a conscious awareness and realization—really more than that, a conscious feeling of the presence of God if you are to avail yourself of that Presence and Power. Glib talk, quotations, hearsay, and metaphysical clichés are not to be confused with that conscious awareness and realization through which God becomes a living reality to you. An indulgence in metaphysical clichés is as useless as it would be for someone living in ancient times to say, "You know, electricity is available." Yes, of course it was—if they had known how to make use of it.

This talking about God has been going on for thousands of years, and there are many godly people in churches who are talking about God and still going through all the discords of human experience. It is not talk, however, but the conscious realization of the presence of God which is the secret of spiritual living.

Anyone who has had the actual feeling, or realization, of the presence of God, is no longer alone in the world, no longer working out his own problems alone, and no longer dependent on human aid of any kind. Always the Divine is there. The Presence that goes before him is always beside him and comes up behind him as a rearguard, but even though there is such a Presence, there must be a conscious realization of that Presence.

Toward the development of that state of consciousness there are certain practices which are steps along the way. The most important of these is training yourself to make a conscious effort to realize God's presence upon awakening in the morning. If you cannot feel God's presence immediately, you can at least learn to acknowledge the omnipresence, omnipotence, and omniscience of God; you can at least attempt to realize: *As the wave is one with the ocean, so I am one with God. As the sunbeam is one with the sun, so I am one with God.*

If you will take one or two or three minutes to do this, you will find that you are in a different frame of mind when you step out of bed onto the floor. When you learn not to get out of bed until you have established your conscious oneness with God, your day will begin aright.

When I awaken in the morning, I am in the habit of establishing this conscious realization of the presence of God. I consider that the most important part of my daily work because when I have done that, I have not much to do the rest of the day except look over my shoulder and watch God at work.

Every day, you should religiously follow the instructions in the chapters on "Meditation" and "Prayer" in *The Infinite Way*.[4] For example, when you leave your home in the morning, do not go out the door without consciously realizing that the Presence has gone before you and the Presence remains behind to bless those who pass that way. Do not go out without consciously doing this because your conscious effort determines your demonstration.

In the same way when you sit down to your table, do not eat until you have at least blinked your eyes and silently said, "Thank You, Father!" This is not said in any orthodox sense of grace, but in a very modern metaphysical sense of grace. It is an acknowledgment of God as the source of your supply, an acknowledgment that it was not your own human effort that brought the food to you, and that of yourself you can do nothing; the Father within you has placed this food before you.

There is no way to jump from being a human being to being a spiritual being, but little by little, we must begin to spiritualize our thought until we find ourselves in the kingdom of heaven. We must learn that regardless of what we are doing throughout the day, it is only because of the presence of God that we are doing it. Jesus said, "I can of mine own self do nothing[5] . . . the Father that dwelleth in me, he doeth the works."[6] And Paul said, "I live; yet not I, but Christ liveth in me."[7]

You must see that every bit of good you ever do or experience is the Christ acting in and through you; it is the Spirit of God activating you. The healing activity is the activity of divine Consciousness, the activity of the Christ of your own being, which takes place within you.

~ 2 ~

TEACHER, STUDENT, AND TEACHING

The relationship between teacher and student is a very sacred one and is not dependent upon any degree of human learning that a teacher may possess. Whatever knowledge a spiritual teacher may have acquired will be of very little benefit to his student because what the teacher transmits to the student is his spiritual integrity and uplifted consciousness. Without these he has nothing to give. Libraries are filled with books containing the accumulated knowledge of the ages, and if books alone were a sufficient means of instruction, there would be no need for teachers. But for the most part, those seeking knowledge and inspiration have found that there is something which books cannot convey, something which can only be imparted from person to person. That intangible something is spiritual consciousness.

Therefore, it is the responsibility of a teacher or practitioner to maintain his spiritual integrity, to live up to his highest sense of his own teaching and his own understanding. No one can live any higher than his understanding, but it is possible to sink below the level of that understanding. It is possible to violate one's own integrity, to know the spiritual truth and not live it; but in that case even if a teacher is preaching the deepest of truths, he will not succeed in the teaching of them. On the other hand, if he is living up to his highest sense of spiritual integrity, and if he never said as much as a single word to his student or patient, nevertheless, that person, if he is spiritually ready, will receive illumination. That is spiritual law.

A teacher must always feel an obligation to support and help his student spiritually as long as there is any need for such spiritual support. There should be a willingness and a readiness to reach out and give the student help through an interview, a telephone call, letter, or whatever form his need may take, but the student or patient also has a responsibility not to make a nuisance of himself and to keep his requirements and demands on a legitimate plane.

As long as the teacher maintains his spiritual integrity, the student should uphold his teacher. If the teacher falls from grace, the student should stand by with the teacher and lift him up until it becomes evident that the teacher has no desire to be lifted up. Then the student should find his own way and let his own path to heaven be revealed. If a student falls from grace, a teacher should also stand by until the student makes it clear that he does not want the help of the teacher and has no intention of changing his ways. When that happens, the teacher should feel free to sever the relationship.

The teacher at all times must make it clear that the object of spiritual teaching is to set the student free, free even of the teacher, free in his own Christhood. Therefore, the teacher must be careful not to encourage the student to live at his feet and thereby develop a dependence on him, although the student should never hesitate to call upon the teacher for help to lift him to a place where he becomes independent and is able to walk on the water himself. Unless the student is set free, there is a repetition of what happened with Jesus and his disciples when the Master finally had to say to them: "If I go not away, the Comforter will not come unto you."[1]

The Ancient Wisdom

The teaching of the Infinite Way is as ancient as ancient days. It is presented herein as given by Christ Jesus, and it represents my understanding of spiritual law and truth as revealed by Jesus of Nazareth and his beloved disciple, John. But only those who are on this level of consciousness will be drawn to this message. "My sheep hear my voice."[2]

The foundation of this teaching is oneness, the oneness of God and man as expressed by Jesus when he said, "I and my Father are one."[3] The message stands literally on the truth of the First Commandment, which is that there is but one power, one presence, one life, consciousness, Soul, or Spirit; and this truth is the principle of individual being.

God is the only substance of creation, the law and substance of all form. What we behold with the five physical senses is but the human or limited concept of that which actually is there. Even a good or healthy appearance is but a false sense of reality. We can never see or hear God's creation with the material senses; but with spiritual sense, we can discern the man and universe of God's unfoldment of Its own being, which is interpreted as creation.

The world does not accept the revelation, or the truth, of one power. The world gives power to climate, germs, food, stars, and countless other effects, but no effect of itself is, or has, power. Consciousness—life and truth—is the power unto every effect.

The teaching of one God is never popular with human beings, and so throughout the centuries the idea of one power alternately ascends or recedes in consciousness. Abraham, who can be placed about 1550 B.C. or at the latest 1450 B.C. and who became known as the father of the Hebrews, taught the one God, and this same revelation of God as one Presence and one Power came to King Amenhotep IV of Egypt by way of India, who took from his people their many gods and replaced these with the one God. Eventually, however, Amenhotep was deposed and the many gods of his people restored. Then somewhere between 200 and 800 A.D. this teaching of oneness again appeared in its fullness and simplicity as the Advaita teaching of India. In it, the great mystic, Shankara, revealed the illusory nature of the sense world, and the nature of God as the *I,* or *I Am,* the oneness of God and man which he sums up as *I Am That.*

Jesus of Nazareth's complete demonstration of oneness came with his sublime message: "I and my Father are one. [4] . . . Son, thou art ever with me, and all that I have is thine"[5]–all that God is, I am. That evil is not real, Jesus proved through his healing of the sick, raising from the dead, feeding the multitudes, and, finally, in his own rising above all sense testimony into the revelation of eternal life.

Again, this age is being presented with that same ancient wisdom. The foundation of this teaching is that every person individualizes all the qualities and activities of God–all intelligence, eternal life, all love, all truth. Not one quality is lacking in any individual. The very oneness of the individual with the invisible Universal constitutes the oneness of the individual with every God-created being and idea in the world.

Another phase of the teaching is the nature of error, which I consider of equal importance to an understanding of the nature of God, because unless the unreal nature of what is appearing to us as sin, disease, lack, and war is perceived, we cannot deal with those problems successfully and thus reverse the pictures they present. The failure to understand the nature of error may result in blind faith healing, which often is not permanent.

If there were not something producing a problem in our experience, there would be no problem. We may say, "The problem is not real. I know it is not real." But what good will it do us to know that the problem is not real if it is still going to annoy us as if it were? We must reach a place in consciousness where we know what to do with this nothingness called evil, how to overcome it, dispel it, and get free of it. It *is* nothing. That is true. The spiritual revelation of the nature of error is true: It is nothing—but it remains a problem until we have really come into the awareness which makes it nothing in our experience.

So let us say that the teaching is composed of the letter of truth and the spirit of truth. The letter of truth consists of two parts: first, the nature of God and the relationship of God and man; and second, the nature of error and what to do about it. That is all there is to this teaching so far as the letter of truth is concerned. There are no observances of any kind—no rites, no ritual, no dogma, no formulas—nothing more nor less than understanding the nature of God and the nature of error, and your individual application of it.

The letter of truth is an important part of this teaching, and a knowledge of it is necessary to prevent the student from falling into a blind faith and a belief that somewhere, somehow, there is a God ready and willing to do something for him.

The most important part of this work is gaining the spirit of truth, the actual consciousness of God as ever-present, whether we understand It as an ever-present Father, Law, Guide, or Support. How we interpret God depends on our individual background and temperament. God is ever-present, but even though we are the individualization of all that God is, nevertheless, as human beings, this God-Being seems to be something separate and apart from us until It makes Itself known within our consciousness as the reality of our own being.

The Teaching of Jesus

The Infinite Way is founded upon the teaching of Jesus who is my authority, and while it is true that much of this teaching can be found in some of the oriental scriptures, which antedate the Christian era by three or four thousand years, in no case has it been so clearly stated or so clearly demonstrated as it was by Jesus. Therefore, while I enjoy reading the ancient scriptures, there is no approach other than that of Jesus that is quite as definite, complete, or easy for students of the occidental world to accept, because Jesus' teaching is really a part of our Western consciousness. Authority for practically everything that the Infinite Way teaches is found in the New Testament, particularly in the Gospel according to John and in the writings of Paul.

The three best known absolute teachings in the world are those of Buddha, Shankara, and Jesus. Buddha's real teaching has been almost completely lost in the religion now calling itself Buddhism. As a matter of fact, it would be almost as difficult to find Buddha's original teaching in most of the Buddhism of today as it would be to find the teaching of Jesus in some Christian churches. In many churches there is an actual and open denial of the Christ-teaching. Think for a moment in how many churches is there found the practice of praying for the enemy? In what church during either World War I or World War II were prayer services held for the enemy? Which church taught the soldiers to pray daily for those who persecuted them? Who taught the members of congregations that those who live by the sword must die by the sword? Who revealed the spiritual significance of Jesus' refusal to let Peter avenge him by cutting off the ear? Who taught the Commandment: "Thou shalt not kill"[6]?

Remember, therefore, that in discussing the teaching of Jesus, it is not the teaching of Jesus as presented through any particular church that is being discussed, but the teaching as found in the New Testament, without anybody's opinion or interpretation, just Jesus' teaching as it is set forth literally by his followers. Only through the development of the spiritual consciousness exemplified by Jesus will all nations finally be enabled to put up their swords and turn them into ploughshares.

You may wonder whether or not anyone can live up to a teaching as demanding as this, but it can be done–it can be done individually and collectively. You can begin now to live up to the Master's teaching by forgiving your enemy and by praying for those who persecute you; and if you, as an individual, can do this, the world can.

One of the greatest laws of the Bible is the law of forgiveness, of praying for your enemies. But forgiveness does not mean looking at a human being, remembering the terrible offense he has committed against you, and then forgiving him for it. There is no virtue in that. True forgiveness is the ability to see through his human appearance to the Divinity of his being and realize that in the Divinity of his being there has never been, and is not now, error of any nature. It is as if this person were to ask you for help, and in helping him you would have to behold him as he really is, as pure spiritual being.

Every day we are called on to look upon all those toward whom we have any negative feeling as spiritual beings and practice this act of forgiveness. This means turning to the Christ of our own being, and there knowing that nothing but love exists. There never has been a mortal being, and all that appears as a mortal is but the Christ Itself incorrectly seen.

Like forgiveness, praying for our enemies is one of the great laws of life and of the Bible. This does not mean that we are helpless before the enemy: It really means being able to understand God as the life and the mind of individual man, and to know that there is no other mind but that one. Appearances have nothing at all to do with it. We are not dealing with appearances. We are dealing with the reality of being.

Oneness, the Keynote

The teaching is that you must individually contact God. God must become real and alive to you in your experience, and the purpose of this entire work is raising consciousness to that point. "And I, if I be lifted up from the earth, will draw all men unto me."[7]

The moment that I make the contact and feel the presence of God, in that moment, all those within range of my consciousness must feel it and be lifted up. Ultimately they are lifted up to that height where they themselves make the contact and have the realization for themselves. If there is any secret in this teaching, it is that in the degree in which you can open your consciousness to the inflow of the presence of God, to the awareness of God or the Christ, in that degree do you practice and ultimately demonstrate it.

The Infinite Way is not another metaphysical approach designed to get rid of disease, to demonstrate an automobile or health, or to acquire any material thing. Following this path involves a willingness to take no thought for your life, for the things that you eat or drink, or wherewithal you shall be clothed. It is an attempt to seek the consciousness of God and let these things be added. It is not possible to have the consciousness of God and any kind of lack, the consciousness of Infinity and an absence of something. So, in attaining the consciousness of the presence of God, you likewise attain all the added things—all those things which are in, and of, God.

The highest demonstration was expressed by Jesus when he said: "I can of mine own self do nothing[8] . . . the Father that dwelleth in me, he doeth the works."[9] I am sure that Jesus did not mean that there were two people, Jesus and the Father. When he used the term, "Father," he meant the divine essence, presence, or law of the Infinite. That is what he meant by his use of the word, Father, and that is our meaning also.

In acknowledging God, or a divine Father, we are not acknowledging some Person or even some Being or Power outside ourselves. That would be two-ness. That would be duality and would be fatal. We acknowledge:

*I am the only one. "I and my Father are one," and I am that
one. This that I feel coursing through me is the Father, and It is
greater than I, greater than my humanhood.*

"I live; yet not I, but Christ liveth in me." When Paul
made that statement, he was not thinking of a man
named Jesus or of some kind of a separate being within
him. He understood and knew that he meant the Christ,
the Messiah, the Savior, the Essence, the Power, the
Law, the Presence.

True, It has the strength and power and dominion of
a father, the love and tenderness of a mother, and the
understanding of a friend. But more than that, It is a
Presence that cannot be defined. That is where the
difficulty lies—trying to express the Indefinable in words.
Lao-tze said: "If you can define it, it is not God." If you
could ever describe this Thing, you would not be describing God because God is infinity, eternality, immortality, and no one can describe that. You can feel It,
become conscious of It, aware of It—but you cannot
describe It.

One Power, a Basic Principle

Another fundamental point in this teaching which
may be difficult to grasp in its fullness but which is very
simple once its meaning is caught is the teaching of one
power. The First Commandment is the platform on
which we stand: Thou shalt have no other powers but
Me; there is no other power but God—there is no sin to
overcome, no death, no lack, no limitation, no temptation. The only Power, the only Presence, is God. Truth
is not used to overcome error; the power of God is not

used to overcome evil, and when universal belief, in the form of sin, disease, death, lack, and limitation, cries out to us, "I have power to crucify you," we respond as did Jesus, "Thou couldest have no power at all against me, except it were given thee from above."[10]

That treatment which Jesus gave Pilate was a statement of absolute truth, and he demonstrated it. All Pilate's power to nail him to the cross, proved to be an empty nothingness because he could not touch the life of Jesus. And so with us. We stand on the First Commandment. Study the chapter, "The Law," which deals with the Ten Commandments, in *Spiritual Interpretation of Scripture* and see how clearly the light of the one power is revealed.

Give up the idea that truth dispels error. Error is not a reality and does not have to be destroyed. It merely has to be recognized for the nothingness which it is. God, Truth, is the only power. We do not use It: We are It. That which I am seeking, I am.

Many years ago early in my practice, I had a call for help from a woman who was arthritic, and whose teacher, as well as many practitioners, had been unable to do anything for her. In three weeks, I had made just about as much progress with the case as all the others had—there was no improvement whatsoever. Her practitioners were convinced that the case could not be met because the woman had a domineering personality, and they believed that she could not be healed unless she changed her thinking or at least changed certain qualities of her thought. So I knew that it would have to be worked out in another way.

Then came a telephone call that the pain was terrific and that something must be done at once. In my enthusiasm I said to myself, "I will sit up all night and break this!" My habit then was to do a little reading to find something to give impulse to thought, to meditate, take a little nap, and then get up and try again.

At two o'clock in the morning, the thought came to me, "There is a truth, and if I could just lay hold of that truth, it would meet this claim. All I need is just one truth, and it is round about here somewhere! If I can just get it!"

Then I went to sleep and in fifteen minutes awakened and heard a Voice: "That which I am seeking, I am!"

"But how can that be?" I asked. "I am not the truth."

Then I remembered that Jesus had said, "I am the way, the truth, and the life."[11] And I realized, "This truth that I am seeking, I am. That makes it very simple because truth is universal, and if I am the truth, this patient is also the truth. No use sitting up any more."

In the morning a call came that the case had been met, and there has been no sign to this day of any arthritis. There is no relapse when we know the truth, when we do not use truth to overcome error. When we attempt to overcome error with truth, we are acknowledging the power of error, and it may come back in double force and surprise us some day. From that time to this, I have never reached out to try to heal anyone out here or overcome some error, because God is the only power and God is the substance and the law of all form.

Remember, the truth itself does nothing for you! It is *your consciousness of the truth* that makes it work. Truth is always the truth, whether you know it or not, but it manifests itself to you only in proportion to *your conscious awareness of it*. It is like the bank account you know nothing about. Only the bank account you know about can be of any benefit to you. I myself went through a period when even a small sum of money would have been very welcome. At that particular time, I did not know I had any money and then later found two accounts in a New York City bank which had been there for twenty years, but which I had completely forgotten. There were many times when I would have been very grateful for that money. Just as the bank account you do not know you have is of no value to you, so this truth of the allness of God is of no use to you except in proportion as you know it and become consciously aware of it.

This is one of the most important things you will ever be called upon to realize. Only in proportion as you see that disease is not a power to which you do something, can you meet the appearance called disease. This is the point I make: There is only one Power, one Presence. Our good must come through That from within, not through any human attempt to drag it out of the world from the outside.

Treatment Is Always on the Level of God

In this teaching we stand on the principle of the one Life, the one Spirit, permeating all. The appearance called death is not death, and the appearance called birth could never be the beginning of Life. Life has no beginning and no ending. This Life which is God is Self-maintained and Self-sustained and has no opposite and no opposition. There is no power apart from the one Life, which is your life and my life, and that Life is eternal.

The moment we touch the Center, the divine essence of Being within our own being, we have contacted not only God, but the life of individual man, the life of the one calling himself, for the moment, a patient. Treatment then lies in the ability to contact this one Life, our own Soul—this one Essence, this one Being which is within our being—and, therefore, in our form of treatment, it is not necessary to send thought out to a person. On the contrary, that is enough to prevent or delay the healing and in some cases make it impossible.

The correct treatment from the standpoint of Spirit, or Soul, is to go within, to touch the Center of one's own being. Never take the name of the patient there; never take the claim, whether it is one of unemployment, insanity, or disease: Take nothing with you there but God, and God is already there. Find God! And when that sense of release comes, you will soon get word from the patient that he is healed.

This is my word to you after years and years of practice: Do not take the name or the identity or the picture or the thought of your patient into your treatment. Leave these completely outside. You have nothing to do with them. They are illusory to begin with, and if you take them into consideration, obviously you do not believe they are illusions, but think they are something and that you must do something about them. It may be true, perhaps, at times that, because you have a patient, you mistakenly believe for a moment that there is a presence and power apart from God. So you go within for illumination, for the light which will dispel the illusion.

When you turn within, leave the problem outside! The problem should not concern you, whether it be mental, physical, moral, or financial. It has nothing to do with you because you cannot meet a problem on the level of the problem. The problem appears as lack, limitation, unemployment, homelessness, sin, disease, or death, but the moment you begin to do anything about it on that level, you are unable to meet it. Wherever the problem is, the answer is; and if the problem is in your thought, the answer is there also. They are never separated from each other. Always they are one. There is no problem here and an answer to the problem somewhere else.

Therefore, when a problem is presented to you, drop it and turn within until you attain that center of consciousness where you feel the release, and then the whole problem disappears. If you work on the problem, if you work to achieve something, in that moment you have defeated your purpose.

Then how are you to find the center of your being? First of all, turn away from the problem. Forget it. Close your eyes and take some quotation into your thought, preferably a very short one like "I and my Father are one,"[12] or, "Be still, and know that I am God."[13] As you dwell on that quotation and your thoughts begin to wander, wondering what to have for luncheon or what to do tomorrow, pay no attention to them; let them come and let them go.

Keep your attention on "I and my Father are one," or on any other appropriate short quotation from Scripture or spiritual wisdom. As you lose the thread, gently come back to it and recognize that even though your mind has wandered, "I and my Father are one." Bring your attention back again and again, and as many times as you lose that thread, gently bring it back. There is no hurry about it. Just gently come back to "I and my Father are one."

After you have done this for a few minutes, you will find yourself becoming more peaceful. If it is possible then, in that moment of quietness, remember that you are listening for "the still small voice." Keep your ears open as if there were a message just outside waiting to come in.

You are now developing a state of receptivity to "the still small voice." So, as you keep your mind stayed on "I and my Father are one . . . I and my Father are one"; all the time the ear is listening, and a sense of peace is settling down upon you.

Infinite Way treatment is concerned only with your relationship to God, and when you become one with God, you will feel the release. When that release and that sense of peace come, the problem has been met, either your own or someone else's. Your patient will feel the release because he has been brought into your consciousness, and inasmuch as God is the consciousness of the practitioner, God is also the consciousness of the patient. There is no transference of thought from practitioner to patient—there is no need for it.

Never be guilty of an attempt to give a patient a treatment. Do not make the mistake of thinking that a patient goes to a practitioner, who goes to God, and that God then in turn goes to the patient to do the releasing; or that the patient goes to the practitioner, and the practitioner sends something out to the patient. Nothing like that happens.

God and the practitioner and the patient are really one. There are not three and there are not two: There is just one. The more clearly you recognize that *I AM* is God, and that *I AM* is the life and the Soul and the Spirit of every individual, the sooner will you realize that you are not dealing with people, but with God, infinitely and individually expressed *as* people—but still God, only God.

God as Causative Principle

God is all. God constitutes individual being and body. And now comes the next question: "What is God?" One of our greatest problems is to find a satisfactory answer to that question. There are perhaps several hundred synonyms for the word, God, and if we could name all of them we still would not have found the answer to the question. Nevertheless we continue to raise that age-old query, "What is God?" Perhaps that is because there is an inner recognition of which we may not even be aware that when we have found God we have found ourselves, and when we have found ourselves we have found God.

Surely we can all agree that God is the causative principle of the universe. We cannot say, however, that God created the universe because that would mean that at one time there was God and no universe, and then suddenly there was God and a universe. God is not a creator any more than is the principle of mathematics. The principle of mathematics did not create two times two is four; it did not create a four and fasten it on to two times two. Two times two includes four, and as soon as two times two came into being, the four was there. The principle of mathematics did not put it there; God did not put it there—He could not. It was there. It had never been separated from two times two.

But when we think of God as a creative Principle— infinite, eternal, omnipresent, without beginning and without ending—then we can see that a cause must be a cause *of* something, and that something we call an effect. Cause and effect are one, co-existent, co-eternal, and of the same substance. So we arrive at the truth that God, as creative Principle, is the cause of Its manifested being appearing as effect, a cause and effect that are bound together, like two times two is four, not separate from each other, but always in one place.

Dwell on the idea: What is God? Only in the realization of what God is can we know that which God is God to. All we know, we know because we are a state of consciousness. Take away the activity of consciousness, and we would have no awareness, no knowledge. We would not know that we exist.

It was Descartes who said: "I think, therefore I am." Similarly, only because I am conscious, because I am consciousness itself, do I know that I exist and do I know that there is a universe existing. If we can in a measure understand ourselves and understand God as Consciousness, we can understand this universe, including our body, as a formation of Consciousness—incorporeal, spiritual, eternal, co-existent, Self-maintained, and Self-sustained; in fact, as Self-maintained and Self-sustained as the way in which two times two is four maintains itself unto eternity.

When we can see that Consciousness is the reality of our being, that It is causative principle, then we can see that Consciousness forms or becomes evident to us as an infinite variety of forms and is therefore as eternal as we ourselves are. Once we have the understanding that our consciousness is the causative principle of our universe, then we know that, no matter what we do, the universal Consciousness is ever producing and reproducing.

No matter what we do with the world of effect, the Consciousness which is its causative principle, substance, and law is forever producing and reproducing. It is not creating. It is just unfolding, like the moving-picture reel, unfolding the entire picture. The picture is already there on the reel and is only unfolding to our view.

Consciousness is always unfolding and disclosing Itself to us in infinite form, in infinite ways, and in infinite variety. There should be no regrets over our past lives and no regrets over what we have lost in the past. The past has nothing to do with today. We are not dependent on yesterday's manna; we are not dependent on anything or anyone. It makes no difference what has become or what becomes of our fortune or our assets. It is today that our consciousness is revealing to us its new creation, revealing its new formations every day. Today our consciousness is unfolding and disclosing itself in new ways, in new forms—always increasing abundantly.

Biblical Characters as Stages of Individual Unfoldment

The subject of God is an infinite one. It is the most important part of our work, so we shall come back to it again and again, because without a knowledge of God, we can have no knowledge of the effect of God. A close study of the Bible helps to reveal God to us and how God governed the lives of biblical characters.

In *Spiritual Interpretation of Scripture*, it was unfolded that the men and women of the Bible represent qualities of our own thought. For example, we may think of Moses and wonder what quality he represents in our thought. You will remember that he led the Hebrews out of their religious and economic darkness into a more abundant sense of human life, into a greater sense of religious and economic freedom, and into greater territorial expansion. Therefore, Moses must represent a higher type of humanhood.

When first we turn to metaphysical truth, nearly always it is for the purpose of finding a greater sense of religious or economic freedom, or physical freedom in the sense of health—and usually our first demonstrations consist of just such improved humanhood. They are not really the experience of the Christ at all. True, we talk in terms of the Christ and think we are demonstrating the Christ, but in most cases we are not really receiving any spiritual vision. We increase our income from fifty to seventy-five dollars a week or change a sick heart into a healthy one, or a sick lung into a healthy one, and there is no doubt but that we enjoy a greater degree of freedom in our human experience.

There is, then, that Moses-quality in our thought which leads us to truth and ultimately to a greater sense of freedom in our human experience. So, too, the Jesus-quality of thought in our consciousness is that which will lead us out of our human good into spiritual good. It is that which will lead us out of an improved state of humanhood with its increased income or improved health into the realization of our spiritual Selfhood.

The Savior, or Christ, is within our own consciousness. The mind that was in Christ Jesus is the mind of us. When Jesus told us: "Before Abraham was, I am,"[14] and "Lo, I am with you alway, even unto the end of the world,"[15] he was not referring to his humanhood, because that was not here before Abraham and is not here today. But he knew that the *I* of which he spoke, the *I* which is the Christ, was in human consciousness before Abraham and is in our consciousness this minute.

So the very quality we call Jesus, which is the presence of the Christ—the healing or saving Christ—is the quality of our consciousness this moment and is operating while we are awake or asleep. The Christ really is the healing influence. It is what in the Aramaic language was known as the

Messiah, what the Greeks knew as Savior, and what we know as the Christ. The Christ is not a man of two thousand years ago, but a quality of our own consciousness this very moment. And so each character of the Bible is represented in our consciousness as some quality or activity.

As I have discussed in *Spiritual Interpretation of Scripture*,[16] it was quite a revelation to me when I realized that the experience of Joseph, which apparently had been brought on by his brothers, was not really evil, but God Itself driving Joseph into Egypt where he could fulfill his mission. If you could have heard some of the things I have heard from people about the discordant conditions which they have experienced in order to be brought into a realization of what it was necessary for them to know, you would better understand how, throughout Joseph's entire experience, God was appearing as his individual consciousness, leading him to fulfillment.

God always appears as individual consciousness. God in Its infinity is our individual consciousness, and it is our consciousness that contains the entire universe; it is our consciousness that becomes the law unto our world. The very moment that we can consciously feel and realize the presence of the Christ, we have that quality of being which to our sense annihilates every form and belief of sin or erroneous conditions in our experience. The chapters on "Unveiling the Christ" and "Cleansing the Temple" in *Spiritual Interpretation of Scripture* will amplify this point.

The higher we are in spiritual consciousness, the easier it is to discern spiritually what we read. So it is important to be lifted up into a higher consciousness and from there do our reading and thinking. In that way, higher revelations can be unfolded to us.

~ 3 ~

STATES AND STAGES OF CONSCIOUSNESS

Even though for many years the metaphysical world has believed that mental and spiritual healing are synonymous, actually they are as far apart as are material and spiritual healing. Mental and material healing are much the same except that they operate on different levels of consciousness. The mental is a little higher and finer than the material, but essentially they are two strata of the same belief.

On the other hand, to use the terms, "mentally spiritual" or "spiritually mental," is exactly the same as saying, "a godly devil." The spiritual and the mental are just that far apart, not that one is right and the other is wrong, but they function on such different levels of consciousness that they are as far apart as the poles.

The present day mixture of the spiritual and the mental stems from the beginning of modern mental practice, which originated in the last quarter of the eighteenth century in Germany with Franz Anton Mesmer, a reputable and learned physician, who named his discovery animal magnetism. He it was who discovered that there is a vital fluid—invisible and mental—which passes from the practitioner to the patient and which acts hypnotically through suggestion.

One of Mesmer's students, the French mesmerist, Charles Poyen, migrated to Portland, Maine, and there found an apt student named Phineas P. Quimby to whom he taught mesmerism, then known as hypnotism, or animal magnetism, and for some time these two engaged in this activity primarily for entertainment purposes.

Mr. Quimby, later known as Dr. Quimby, however, had a young patient, or student, who worked as his assistant and who developed the faculty, under hypnotism, of discerning the mental causes for the physical diseases of people coming to him on the platform. Dr. Quimby, then, by recognizing the nonpower of the mental thought, erased the disease. As a result of some remarkable healings which took place, he gave up the entertainment phase of his work and became a very well-known healer. People flocked to him from all over the country, and there are reports of amazing healings.

Dr. Quimby was a very good man—a religious man in a church sense—and very soon he began to introduce the words God and the Christ into the terminology of his work. Gradually, these religious terms became a part of what was in the beginning a purely mental practice. As a matter of fact, I believe it was Dr. Quimby who first made the distinction between Jesus and the Christ—Jesus, the man, and Christ, the Spirit that animated him. Up to that time in the theological world, Jesus and the Christ had been thought of as one. In metaphysical language today, however, Jesus is understood to be the man, and the Christ, the power or presence or Spirit of God which animated the man Jesus.

Of all Dr. Quimby's students, the one who became best known was Mary Baker Eddy, who travelled for three years giving lectures for him on the science of Quimbyism, which he later called the Science of Christ, or Christian Science. Because of her religious background, Mrs. Eddy was well-steeped in the Bible and in the religious thought of her day, and she therefore utilized all the religious terms which Dr. Quimby had introduced into his mental practice.

But let us not deceive ourselves: It was a mental practice, so mental that when engaged in the healing work Mrs. Eddy often had to ask Dr. Quimby to help her because she had taken on the disease of the patient she was treating. Early letters which passed between Mrs. Eddy and Dr. Quimby show that the practice in which they were engaged was mental even though they used terms such as the Christ. It was one mind over another mind or mind over matter or one mind understanding that disease is not a power. It was primarily suggestion—the transference of the thoughts of one mind to another.

As time went on, more and more people began to be interested in metaphysical healing, coming into the work through many other avenues. Julius A. Dresser began the New Thought movement in 1892, two years before the original Mother Church in Boston was built. While it is true that most of the students and practitioners adhered closely to the mental approach, others who were of a more spiritual temperament made progress in the spiritual field.

Thus in the metaphysical field, there are two distinct branches—the mental and the spiritual—although very few people are willing to acknowledge that this is true. Nowhere in the New Testament, however, can authority be found for most of what is now known as mental practice, although that mental practice still makes use of the name of the Christ.

"Holding Thoughts" Is Not Spiritual Healing

Jesus taught: "Take no thought for your life, what ye shall eat, or what ye shall drink; nor yet for your body, what ye shall put on,"[1] and yet how many of our mental practitioners today are ready and willing to attempt to make a demonstration of supply or of a house or an automobile? How many patients ask their practitioners to "demonstrate" an apartment or a house in which to live, or a husband or getting rid of one. There is not a practitioner of any experience who has not at times had the very sad experience of having people come to him asking for help to secure a home, an automobile, a husband, or a wife—every kind of "demonstration" conceivable.

Even the highest level of that type of practice is against the teaching of the Christ. The Christ-teaching is to take no thought for your life, for your supply, or for your clothing. Jesus gives a long list of what *not* to ask for, tells why, and ends with this promise: "Your Father knoweth that ye have need of these things. . . . [and] it is your Father's good pleasure to give you the kingdom."[2] Therefore, to go to God with some finite problem would be going against the teachings of the Master.

In Luke, Jesus also said, "Which of you with taking thought can add to his stature one cubit?"[3] When you sit down to "take thought" in order to add something to your supply or your health, you will fail. Furthermore, the Bible states: "For my thoughts are not your thoughts, neither are your ways my ways."[4] Yet think of all the metaphysicians in the world who believe that if they just do some right thinking—hold or send out the right thought—it will do something for them or for their patients, although in practicing this doctrine of "right thinking" they are violating the very teaching which they claim to be following.

The transfer of thought from one individual to another is the activity of the human mind. Although it often results in what we call healing or improvement, it is sometimes at best merely temporary, because if the mental practitioner is successful today, he must work twice as hard next week. What can be the end of all this mental practice but a headache! People who become adept in mental work begin tightening up because they are working under pressure—mental pressure. Some of you may have observed the reaction on those who give or receive mental treatments; you may have watched practitioners who have carried on their work under terrific mental pressure and witnessed the confusion it has brought.

During my sixteen years in the Christian Science practice, I observed that mental practice was just as rife there as it is in other metaphysical movements. As a matter of fact, there is just as much authority in Mrs. Eddy's writings for mental practice as for spiritual practice. Both are taught and can easily be found in her writings, and anyone may take his choice, depending on whichever teaching has the greater appeal for him. Although I personally have never been able to indulge in mental practice, I have seen the results of those who have used it and also the results on those who have permitted themselves to come under the mental treatment of another person "holding thoughts" for them, dominating them and at times almost controlling them.

Those who work without this active thought-taking process remain relaxed. Instead of trying to be a force or power, they merely become the vehicle through which the Spirit works; and therefore, there is seldom any nervousness or irritability because the Spirit is ever renewing and rebuilding. The Spirit is doing the work, not their "thought-taking."

Under the dominion of the Spirit, of that mind that was in Christ Jesus, it would be impossible for anyone to violate his spiritual integrity. No one could cheat, defraud, or be unfaithful in his duty to a patient, because the Spirit would not let him—It would not give him such a thought or impulse. Moreover, when a practitioner comes under the dominion of that mind which was also in Christ Jesus, he heals without mental or personal effort, whether the patient is awake or asleep—and even when the practitioner is asleep.

When a person is working mentally he has the choice of being good or bad, with no controlling power to prevent his doing what he wants to do, except for his own highest sense of right. That does not mean that those working along mental lines are evil people; but if they are good, it is because they are good people, not because they have come under the influence of that mind which was in Christ Jesus, which would permit them to be nothing less than God in action.

No Mental Cause for Disease

How many times have you known someone who was convinced that he had arthritis or cancer or consumption and then was healed so quickly that later he was equally convinced that he could not have had anything seriously wrong with him? Quite possibly the condition was not there, but the point is: Suppose a practitioner accepts the diagnosis as presented to him and begins to work on it. Nine times out of ten he would be working to heal the wrong disease. Even if his patient brought him a doctor's diagnosis, it could still be fifty-five percent wrong. In its own survey, the Massachusetts General Hospital in one year learned that the diagnoses made in its own hospital were but forty-five percent correct, and this even with x-rays, blood tests, urinalyses, and all the other tests devised by modern medicine.

You can see that even if a practitioner were given a medical diagnosis of a case, it might be right or it might be wrong, and if he had no medical diagnosis and just took his patient's word for it, he might be seventy-five to ninety percent wrong. So what good is a treatment given for a specific claim? If the patient gets well, he might have done so in spite of the treatment.

Moreover, since disease is an unreality and since it is a belief that really cannot be localized, all this mental manipulation—this probing to find a mental cause for a condition or a disease—is nonsense.

In my entire life I have never met any person with enough hate in his system to cause anything as virulent as cancer or enough lust to cause consumption or tuberculosis. A person who had that much hate or lust would be locked up in an institution. People are just not that bad—there must be a different reason for it.

Some time ago I read an article about a woman with flat feet. She had had her thought analyzed by a practitioner who discovered that the woman had grieved so over her son who had been killed in the war that she had lost her understanding. Result: flat feet. Another woman had athlete's foot and could not be healed, so her practitioner examined her thought and found that she had a desire for human affection. My comment at that time was that if that is true, practitioners are going to be very busy with cases of athlete's foot when there is so much need for affection in the world.

If there ever was a time when healing was brought about through handling mental causes, take my word for it they were "belief" healings, a belief of disease healed by entertaining a belief of a cause and a cure, one belief acting upon another belief. I have read the New Testament until I have worn out the book and in no place can I find Jesus saying anything about hatred, lust, or a desire for affection causing a disease. Instead, he said, that even sin had not caused a man to be born blind.

It shocked me to learn that error is not the result of a person's thinking because I had always been taught that disease is caused by wrong thinking, but I discovered in the first year of my practice that this is not true. How could a baby suffer because his parents were indulging in wrong thinking? No, he suffers from universal beliefs which his parents do not know how to handle. People do not contract colds, "flu," and polio in their "seasons" because of their wrong thinking: These are universal beliefs which they do not know how to meet, and if they cling only to this God-is-love business without learning how to handle these beliefs, they will be as badly off as if they had never discovered that God is love.

The weakness in metaphysical practice is that most metaphysicians like to talk about how wonderful God is, but dislike intensely telling anyone what to do about the appearance of sin and disease. Would there be a single person experiencing lust, animality, fear, or false appetite, if he knew how to deal with it? There is a law of God that annuls these, but you must know what that law is. Just saying, "God is love," does not do it because we already have too much of that in the world even among people who are sure that God is love.

Never forget that every evil circumstance in your life can be prevented. Nobody is a victim of anything but his ignorance of the laws of life. God never intended anyone to suffer from old age; God never intended that there be cripples, alcoholics, or drug addicts, and there is no reason in the world why there are, except that the world has never learned how to meet these problems and destroy them in human belief.

Evil does not exist as a God-created thing. God does not punish people even though the old Hebraic law taught that the sins of the fathers shall be visited upon the children. When the Hebrews saw how unjust such a law was, however, they rescinded it two hundred years later: ". . . they shall say no more, The fathers have eaten a sour grape, and the children's teeth are set on edge."[5] Yes, they learned three or four thousand years ago not to accept such a cruel idea as that the sins of the fathers are visited upon the children, and certainly we should be at least that far advanced. And yet we have accepted laws of heredity which bind us to the belief that the ills of the father are visited on the children, the grandchildren, and the great-grandchildren. We must rise higher than that, and we can make a beginning by understanding that there is a law of God in operation in individual and collective being, in individuals and in groups, races, and nations.

Thought Is Not Power

There is a law of God, but we have to begin to bring that law into operation, first, by giving up our egotistical beliefs that any kind of thinking we can do is a power, or that taking a statement and drilling it into our mind will finally make it come true. Maybe it will come true. But that is hard work; it is neither permanent nor spiritual; and furthermore, it permits others to dominate our thoughts and also takes away from us our realization of the only Power there is, which is God, whose kingdom is within us.

Repeating that two times two is four will not make it so, though it might help us to remember that it is so. The repetition of an affirmation will help to impress us with its truth, but it would be far better to hear or read a truth, and better still to have Truth revealed from within our own being and let that Truth do the work, since Truth is really a synonym for God. Why depend upon the manipulation of Truth? Why not let Truth do it alone?

How many people are there who really and truly believe that there is a God? Oh, yes, they accept God and talk about Him. But how many of those who claim to believe in God at the same moment cling to a medicine or to a thought? Neither the medicine nor the thought can ever be God. God is not thought. Thought is not God-power: *Thought is an avenue of awareness.* That is one statement you might memorize, not in order to make it come true, but if ever you should be tempted to manipulate thoughts, remembering that statement will bring you sharply to the realization that no amount of thinking is power.

When the truth came to me that thought is not a power, but only an avenue of awareness, I was startled for a moment. Then I saw that through my thought—through the avenue of thought—I could become aware of people around me and know whether they were dressed in brown or green or black, but no amount of thinking I could do could change the brown to green or the green to black. Not my thought, nor all the thought in the world, could change that. Thereafter, for me, thought became an avenue of awareness.

Through thought, you can become aware of the great truth that you are the Christ of God. That is what you are and have been since time began. It has always been true. "Before Abraham was, I am"[6] and nobody's thinking that can make it true. It is true because it is a law of God. "Lo, I am with you alway"[7] even unto the end of this human belief of things. That *I* will be with you and that *I* is the Christ, the mind that was in Christ Jesus, the Soul, or Spirit, of God.

One grain of the Christ does miracles when left to operate without mental manipulation, without the mental desire to reach out to the consciousness or the mind or thought of the individual seeking help. How many times have you had the experience of being in an office with a practitioner of highly developed spiritual consciousness and feeling some beneficial effect, some uplift, or some sense of peace? But do you believe it is necessary to be in the same room or in the actual presence of the practitioner to have that experience? Does the body or the brain have anything to do with it? No, you could sit in your home in China and receive the same divine impulse from any individual in whom the mind of Christ is even in a tiny measure in the ascendancy.

Availability of the Mind That Was in Christ Jesus

We must go further than mind science and mental healing, and come to that place where we work in accordance with the revelation or teaching of Christ Jesus. Jesus lived "not by might, nor by power, but by my spirit."[8] Is there any better way to heal than that, or any way that will leave your patient freer to function normally without undue influence from other human beings? "Not by might, nor by power, but by my spirit," by *My Spirit,* the Spirit of God, by that mind which was also in Christ Jesus, which is not only the mind of the Christ, but the mind of you and the mind of me.

The mind that was in Christ Jesus is as available to you today as if Jesus were sitting in this room. If you do not believe that this is true, try this experiment: Sometime when you are feeling tired or ill and have the opportunity to be by yourself, close your eyes and ask yourself whether the mind that was in Christ Jesus was inside his brain or inside his body, or was he stating a profound truth when he said: "Before Abraham was, I am.[9] . . . Lo, I am with you alway, even unto the end of the world.[10] . . . If I go not away, the Comforter will not come unto you."[11]

If you believe those words to be the truth, you will relax in this realization: "All right! Mind of Christ Jesus, Father within, the Christ! As long as You are with me, I can sit back and rest in peace!" Then rest in that peace and see if you do not have an instantaneous healing without "taking thought."

At first you may not be healed of your more serious claims and problems because most of us are still in that place where we might not be able to accept such healings without thinking we had seen a "miracle." But begin in small ways with the lesser problems. Rest in the mind that was in Christ Jesus and see if it is not as available to you here and now as if Jesus were in the room.

Regardless of where the practitioner is, you are not going to reach out to him as a person, but to the mind that was in Christ Jesus, which is the mind of the practitioner. You must never limit yourself to the human mind of any person. The mind of Christ Jesus realized is the mind of you and of me, available to all, whether close or far. That is the secret of living in Christ-consciousness, the secret of the Infinite Way. Paul's statement, "I live; yet not I, but Christ liveth in me,"[12] is true, and every time anyone reaches out to a person of realized Christ-consciousness, he is reaching out to the Christ, which is living through and as that person.

Be grateful that every truth is a universal truth, not only about Jesus Christ, but about everyone in the world who will open his consciousness and accept it—accept it, not about a human being, because a human being is limited to his human, educated mind or to his experience, personality, and birth, but accept it about any individual who will open his consciousness and recognize, "Yes, anything that was true of Moses, Elijah, Elisha, Jesus, John, or Paul is true of me. Otherwise it would not be truth, but only personal sense."

Therefore, if you want to have that mind that was in Christ Jesus continuously, open your consciousness. You need not exercise mental power; you do not have to direct your thought to a certain part of the body or to a certain cause for the disease or to any person, because error is not in any person's body or thinking.

The minute you begin to know that the mind that was in Christ Jesus is your mind, from that moment on, it is doing something to your body, your business, your income, and your human relationships. It may seem slow in the beginning, unless you experience a tremendous light such as Saul had when he became Paul. In that case, it might be quick; but even with Saul, it was nine years after he had had his great experience before he became Paul and went out on his first mission. It took that long for the truth to digest, unfold, and come forth.

So with us. Sometimes we catch a tremendous light but may not understand its full significance until some time later. I noticed this in the early days of my healing practice when I was sending out a weekly letter. Even though I knew the truth of what I wrote, it was only on re-reading those letters two years later that I understood certain statements and felt an inner conviction, or realization, of them.

You will find this to be your experience also because many truths with which you intellectually agree today may only register with you one or two years from now. Often it takes time to rise from the level of egotistical sense to a higher consciousness. If you were at a high enough point of spiritual consciousness, what you have read so far in this book would lift you into heaven. But the fact is that one statement registers with one person here and some other statement with another one there. These words are coming through from the Spirit, but it takes a degree of spiritual awareness to be able to digest and grasp them. Often I find that many statements I have made on different occasions startle me when I hear them again, and I wonder where I ever got that.

Living in "My Kingdom"

One statement from Jesus, "My kingdom is not of this world,"[13] has been my life and my blood and my bones for many years. After having been told that "My kingdom is not of this world," what would you think of me if I began to do some mental work for next month's rent? What would you think of a person who, after having been told that the Christly kingdom has nothing to do with this world, went around worrying about whether he was married or single? If those things are not a part of this world, I do not know what is! It is true that in one sense, we are always in the world, but not in it and of it in the sense that we have any concern for it: We let it unfold—its people and things—and become a part of our being, normally and naturally.

To illustrate: You are reading this book, and yet perhaps in the very room in which you are sitting is a radio or a television, only waiting the turn of a knob to bring you every manner of entertainment—low comedy or inspiring drama, rock and roll or symphony. But you are reading a book on spiritual living! Ask a few thousand or a few dozen people if anything in the world could be more boring, duller, or more uninteresting than such reading.

Then why do you like it? Why do you spend your time doing this? Because you are already living in a different world from that of most people, and it has not been necessary for you to die to get there. One spiritual quotation, one spiritual thought gives you more joy than the most spectacular moving picture. Why? Because you are no longer in a world where that is the measure of your joy. You have left that world—not through the act of dying or of doing anything ridiculous like stopping eating or giving up the wearing of clothes, not through anything of an eccentric nature. And yet you have left that world.

Take another illustration: How many thirty-five cent thrillers and crime novels do you imagine were sold in our country today? Yet here you are, instead of paying thirty-five cents for one of those, you pay three dollars and ninety-five cents for this book! What is wrong with you? Nothing! You are simply living in a different world. You have left that other world.

Another thing, how many people are there who actually believe they cannot make a good honest living without doing a little chiseling or cheating or without using some political influence? You, however, have learned that there is a principle at work within you which enables you to live completely in accord with the law of Christ Jesus, with the law laid down in the Golden Rule, and you can adopt a principle such as that for yourself and be abundantly cared for—and I mean abundantly—if you want to make the effort to claim it.

That is what I mean by living in a different world. There are those who could never agree that human ingenuity, physical force, mental pressure, and unlimited capital are not necessary. But you know that by the application of spiritual principles you can live a normal and harmonious life, attracting to you all that is a part of your fulfillment. You can experience this fulfillment not through affirmations, but by realizing: *My oneness with God constitutes my oneness with every spiritual idea, and that spiritual idea will express itself as home, friend, student, patient, book, or teacher—anything of which I have need.*

You do not have to go about demonstrating things. You need only demonstrate your oneness with God by opening your consciousness to that truth, accepting it, and letting it become part of your consciousness. Then that truth does the work.

The moment that you begin taking thought for anything in the world that can be known through the physical senses, you are taking thought for this world, and "My kingdom is not of this world." In dealing with the problems of your personal life, you may be doing mental work for right activity, business, supply, companionship, or marriage–all the time having in your mind some particular location where all this must take place. Yet right at this very moment your demonstration may be in Africa, but in outlining the manner and method in which you want your life to unfold, you have closed your whole mind to the direction in which fulfillment lies because Africa may not have entered your thought at all.

If, however, instead of taking thought for anything that had to do with person, place, or thing, your entire work had been for the conscious realization of the mind that was also in Christ Jesus, you then might possibly have heard it voiced within, or might have received a letter telling you what was waiting for you in Africa, China, or somewhere else.

In other words, it is sinful to limit. It is sinful to put any kind of mental limitation on your demonstration. How do you know where it is going to be, when, or with whom? If there is a God governing His own universe, how can you and I have the presumption to limit or outline that demonstration? The truth is that we have no right to outline. We have the right only to abide in the principle of spiritual living which is to take no thought for our life.

The Body Is Life Formed

The telephone bell rings, and a voice cries, "Work for life; I am dying"; but the Bible says: "Take no thought for your life."[14] So my response to that call is, "Yes, I will work to realize God." Life is a synonym for God. Can you not see that if you do any mental work for life, you are probably thinking in terms of life as the opposite of death, but since God is the only life, life has no opposite?

A practitioner once said to a patient, "There is no life in your body"; but the patient naturally wanted to manifest life more abundantly, if not in, then certainly as a body. Too many of us are trying to get rid of our body, denying the body. Can you picture what we would look like without a body? Do not deny the body or throw it away; it is very good to have. You have a body and God gave it to you—not your parents. Not one of you who is a parent knows enough to make a body. God forms the body, not parents, or as I once said to a mother, "At best, you were the oven in which your child was baked."

God is Spirit and expresses Itself infinitely and individually and has Its own way of producing Its image and likeness. This which we see is only our concept of an already divine activity. Human parentage, or so-called human creation, is not spiritual; it is not of God. If it were, everyone would be harmonious and normal, and there would be no diseased or deformed children. It is only because we have left God out of it that we have such conditions.

Most people look upon this experience of human birth as if it were just an animalistic thing. That is a false interpretation. It is not animalistic: It in itself is divine and wonderful. It is we who turn it into something of an animal nature. We must learn to reinterpret it. And when we learn to do that, there will be more happy marriages and fewer divorces.

The only reason for divorce is that a man and a woman see one another merely as man and woman. It is a hard thing for a man and a woman to live together for many years unless there is a common meeting ground, and even more important, a spiritual bond. If only, long before marriage, they could come to the realization that they are not seeking marriage or home or companionship, but are really seeking the presence of God in visible form, there would be more happy marriages, and every child born of such a union would then be God made manifest.

Immortality, Not Longevity

So we come to this point: What is the motive for your study? On that depends your future in this work. I do not mean that those of you who cannot grasp what I am saying may not go back to the mental level again. If necessary, that is what you will have to do until you are able to rise to the spiritual level. But to those of you who have caught a glimpse of the meaning of spiritual living, the whole of your future is going to depend on whether or not you can determine to seek only the consciousness of the presence of God and be satisfied to let the *things* be added. The extent to which you are able to do this will be the measure of your demonstration.

Is your motive in this study merely to change sickness into health, loneliness into companionship, or homelessness into a home? Or, are you ready, at this moment, to stop taking thought for the things of this world which do not belong to the spiritual kingdom and honestly pray: *All I want is the kingdom of God on earth. All I desire is the reign of God in my individual experience, the government of God in my individual affairs.*

When we reach that point, we are seeking the kingdom of God and His rightness, not our sense of rightness—more dollars, more companionship, more health—but *His* rightness, the spiritual sense of good. If we understood the spiritual sense of supply, we would find it to be far different from our present sense of it, just as the spiritual sense of health is far different from the human standard which allots sixty or seventy years as the normal span of life. But His rightness—His standard of supply, His standard of health—would enable us to live abundantly on earth as long as we desired, or as long as we did not get lonesome for those who had gone on before us.

There are people living on earth today who are said to be two hundred years of age, and one man reputedly over six hundred years of age. Such advanced years are possible if the desire is for the spiritual sense of God, health, and immortality—not merely for the physical sense of health or life or longevity.

Is immortality merely living a long time? Is it merely longevity? No, immortality is life eternal without beginning or ending. No spiritual seeker would believe that his consciousness can come to an end even though he might believe that it is inevitable that his body will drop away. But that is a thought which should be corrected at once. Your body does not drop away or age unless you permit it to do so. You are the one who must make the conscious decision that life is eternal and that your body, the temple of the living God, is under the jurisdiction of that life.

Since life is eternal and life is consciousness, how can consciousness be dead? The continuity or life can be understood when you realize that through your own consciousness of being you have existed eternally and that you will exist eternally. In your inner enlightenment, you can go on existing without that moment of passing, that transfer, which the world calls death but which is only *transition.* When you can make the transition out of the world of mortal beliefs, you have made the transition from "this world" into the world of spiritual reality in which you live without taking thought.

Living by "My Spirit"

Let no one believe that living without taking thought has anything to do with becoming a mental blank. On the contrary, the moment you learn to live without taking thought, you will be the most mentally active person in the community because then you are not governed by your own limited sense of mind. The mind that was in Christ Jesus begins to function as you: If you want to write, you will be a writer; if you want to paint, you will be a painter, because there will be no more limitation.

You do not become a mental blank and you do not live in a vacuum, but you are so animated by this spiritual consciousness that even when you are sleeping you are thinking. You are not taking thought which is quite a different thing, but you are receiving divine impulses through the mind, your avenue of awareness, which interpret themselves to you as thought, and you are continuously aware of an infinitely expanding experience.

Never believe that living without taking thought will lead to laziness of any kind. Rather does it bring such activity into life, the wonder is that you ever go to sleep. There is no end to the activity that comes to the person whose being is animated by the Christ-mind. When that Christ-mind takes over in your experience, inspiring and creative thoughts, the thoughts of God—God's thoughts pouring out as man—are flowing forth from you instead of your digging around in your brain for some used-up thoughts or cold truths.

And what is a cold truth? A cold truth is something you remember as a quotation, something which comes to you out of stored-up memory. When a thought comes to that consciousness which is receptive and open, it comes as a hot truth, a live truth, and it carries with it healing or brings with it inventiveness and new ideas. That is what happens when we receive a direct impartation from the divine Consciousness.

A person can dig into all the old books from ages past—and these truths really go back a long way—but the truths found in them will be of no value until they find lodgment in an open consciousness, at which time they become alive. Therefore, the most important aspect of this teaching is not imparting knowledge or giving out statements of truth because every statement I am giving you now has been known throughout the ages.

The real value of this teaching is to develop in you a state of spiritual receptivity, so that you can be receptive to the Christ-mind; to open your consciousness, so that you can receive these truths; to open your consciousness to the inflow of the Christ, so that your open consciousness becomes the living Christ, and thereby becomes the light of the world.

Many people believe that soon there will be another coming of the Christ, but I am convinced that you and I are that coming in proportion as the Christ is awakened in us. Every one of us is now coming into that state of consciousness where we can accept Jesus' statement that the Comforter will come to us when we stop relying on people and human modes and means. When we can open up our consciousness to the whole infinite Christ, then Christ, the Christ of the second coming, will come to you and to me. I cannot believe, though, for a minute, that any second coming of the Christ will be experienced by the person who has taken no time to learn to know the Christ.

We must *experience* the Christ, not by hearsay but by actual demonstration, by actual contact. Some students know that such an experience is possible, and in working with those of receptive thought, I have observed that I can lift them to where they can see the same vision that I see—not through the transference of thought, but through their own individual unfoldment. They have heard "the still small voice" and received impartations through developing their capacity to meditate.

Watch the presence of God open your consciousness to the inflow of good. Do not outline in what form it will appear, through or with whom, or where or when. Open your consciousness to God and let It become evident or manifest—not with mental work, not by repetition or affirmation, "not by might, nor by power, but by my spirit."

~ 4 ~

THE NATURE OF ERROR

God is all, but nevertheless, every day and almost every hour of every day we are faced with error in some form, and if we are to be free of these errors, it is necessary for us to understand the nature of error. Eventually in our meditation, we will become so consciously one with God that error will never come near us; it will fade away automatically even as we approach it. Until that time, however, let us not hesitate or fear to talk about the nature of error and what to do about it when we see evidences of it.

Everyone, regardless of what branch of metaphysics he has studied, has accepted, if only intellectually, the unreal nature of error. Therefore, in the working out of problems it becomes necessary for us to gain as much understanding as possible of the unreal nature of error so that it can be met and dissolved instantaneously.

Error Is Never a Person, Place, Thing, or Condition

Always when error appears to us, it appears as a person, place, thing, or condition. It may appear as disease, that is, as some kind of a localized condition, and that is what fools us. We go to work on the condition, and thereby make it a reality. *Error never appears as error:* It always appears in some form that will ensnare the unwary. If error would only appear as error, all of us would be free. If it would only say to us, "Steal a diamond ring," or, "Commit adultery," we would be so safe from it, because we would never succumb to such temptations. But it never appears in such ways. It always appears as a brilliant diamond attracting us, as a strong, handsome man or a beautiful, alluring woman tempting us. And we do not realize that that apparently desirable form is error. All that we see is the beautiful form that error has assumed, that error appears to be, that error appears *as*.

The metaphysician who is wise and alert, however, will not only recognize that error always appears as person, place, thing, or condition, but that good also appears as person, place, thing, or condition; and every time he sees any form of good—a good person, a generous, kindly, or philanthropic one—he will instantly recognize, "This is God. These are the qualities of God appearing in or as or through this person." If the metaphysician is able to reinterpret or translate even the good forms, he will not get tangled up in personality. He will not be so attached to any person that the loss of that person might almost drive him mad or the fall from grace of any person might so disappoint him as to cause heartbreak.

Even while appreciating a good person, we must look behind the form and recognize that it is God appearing as some form of good. It is really the presence of Love expressed. We do not express this verbally, but that is the consciousness in which we must live.

When I look out at an audience, I know that all that is actually there is God, but God appearing as persons and God appearing as cooperation, love, joy, peace, and dominion. It is all God appearing *as*—God appearing as person, as friend, as teacher, as student; God appearing as light, truth, and love in all Its infinite and individual forms. Everything of a good nature that appears to us should immediately be translated, "I recognize thee, who thou art: Thou art the very presence of God appearing to me as good."

But, on the other hand, we must be equally alert when error appears. Error is not a person. Error is never a person, and to work on an evil or disagreeable person is to become so involved in the human scene that we may have a hard time bringing out a healing. In the same way, error is never a diseased person, even though it appears that way. Therefore, if we work on the disease or the person, we shall find that our healing work is not satisfactory.

When confronted with an evil person or situation or with a sick person, we must learn to translate this person or condition into impersonal error, just as we learn to translate the good person into God.

Take as an illustration the coming together of streetcar tracks: You see the tracks coming together, but because you know that the streetcar tracks do not come together, but only look as if they do, you are able immediately to recognize that appearance as illusion. You know there is no such condition; you know that what you are seeing is merely an optical illusion; and so you are able at once to wipe out any fear of the wrong condition of the tracks or any sense of danger there might be.

All Error Is Hypnotism

Let me call to your mind the illustration of the hypnotist in a vaudeville act whose subject has been induced to believe that he is being followed by a white poodle. As a member of the audience, you know that if you attempted to help the subject rid himself of his white poodle, you would be in the same state of mesmerism in which he is. But because you are not hypnotized, you know that there is no white poodle there. The claim is not a white poodle; the claim is hypnotism. The minute you know that, the man is free. Why is he free? Because the error has been uncovered; it has been seen, it has been recognized, for its *nothingness.* Hypnotism cannot produce a white poodle. It can only produce an illusory appearance of a white poodle.

Just as the hypnotist on the platform makes his subject believe in the presence of a white poodle or some fantastic object, so the hypnotism in "this world" would make us all believe in, and accept, the appearance of evil people, places, conditions, or circumstances. However, if in reality there is any such condition, rest assured there is no God.

Do not ever believe that there is an infinite power called divine Love and at the same time sin or disease in the world. You cannot have both. You have to make your choice. Either you come into the realization that there is a God, a Principle of the universe, or you will be battling sin, disease, and death all your life. But when you see that God is the substance, the law, and the form of all being, then you must also agree that sin, disease, death, lack, limitation, unemployment, and homelessness—all of these—are illusion.

Throughout the centuries human sense has built up what can be termed *materia medica* beliefs, theological beliefs, and other materialistic beliefs, which have become so strong that they act upon people in somewhat the same manner in which hypnotism acts upon the unwary. In other words, you go out into the wind or sit in a draft and catch cold. Why? The wind or the draft cannot give you a cold. A physician admitted to me, after he had thought about it, that the body does not know whether it is out in the open air, in a tightly closed room, or whether the air is a draft coming in through a window or door. If the body is not aware of this, it must catch cold because the mind in some way has accepted that kind of a law.

But you may counter and claim that a newborn baby placed in a draft can catch cold. Does that mean that the newborn baby has the thought of a cold, or does it rather mean that this thought is so universal and powerful as to be almost mesmeric, impinging itself on that baby almost from the moment it is born, and that thereby the baby becomes the victim of that which it does not even know.

For that reason in this work, we use words which, although inadequate, are up to this stage of our unfoldment the only words I know which describe the real nature of error—words such as "hypnotism," "mesmerism," or "suggestion." From now on, when you see a sinful or diseased person, immediately lift your thought to this realization: "I cannot be fooled by this. That is the appearance, but actually it is nothing but a hypnotic suggestion, a mesmeric suggestion, or a universal belief that is appearing to me as a sick or sinful person." If you can do this, you will have an instantaneous or at least a quick healing.

As you meet with error in your experience—and you are meeting it daily whether in your own body or business or through your patients—you might as well know what it is you are meeting, so that you will know how to deal with it, although when you attain oneness with the Christ-consciousness, you may be able to drop out of your thought entirely any knowledge you may have had as to the nature of error. The knowledge of the nature of error is relatively unimportant when you reach the point where you are completely one with that mind that was also in Christ Jesus, and it may be that some of you even at this moment are on such a high spiritual level that when you close your eyes, go to the center of your being, and find yourself one with God, all phases of error and discord disappear without the word, "error," ever coming into your thought.

Never Treat a Person

As a rule, however, when I am first presented with any form of error, that is, when a patient writes or telephones or comes to my office, I have found it helpful to realize quickly that I am not dealing with a person or a condition: I am dealing only with a suggestion that has found lodgment in my consciousness and would try to make me do something about it. When I have done that, I have done all that is necessary in the way of treatment. After that I can sit down, find my peace at the center of God-consciousness, and go on from there.

But unless the error is recognized as hypnotism first, the temptation may likely come in, "This is a pretty kettle of fish! What am I going to do about a serious disease like this? Or what am I going to do with a person this far gone in sin? Or with this person so close to death?"

This last temptation seems to be particularly strong where elderly people are involved because the temptation of the whole world is to think, "Oh, what can you expect!" It is at that moment that it is necessary to be alert to realize that in the kingdom of God there is no such thing as a newborn baby or an elderly person. From the newest born baby to the oldest individual on earth, there is in reality nothing but the presence of God appearing to you in time and space.

There is nothing but the fullness of God expressing itself, and every one of us must express that fullness. All that the Father has is ours! "Son, thou art ever with me, and all that I have is thine."[1] Was this addressed to a person of any particular age? No, it was addressed to you and to me. So when you are presented with cases of unborn children or newborn children, of middle age or old age, remember that you are not dealing with person, place, or thing. On the positive side, you are dealing with God appearing as individual being, and God is just as much God at one hundred years of age as at ten or twenty. On the negative side, however, you are dealing with appearance, with mortality, with a suggestion of a selfhood apart from God.

Therefore, do not let yourself be trapped into treating a person or a disease or into believing that you are dealing with sick or sinful people. Stop such erroneous practice and watch the miracle. Remember, this is a universal truth, and it must prove itself in your practice.

In the kingdom of God, there is no such thing as error, and so it is useless even to try to account for it. On the contrary, admit that this error is only an appearance coming to you; it is merely a temptation to believe in a selfhood apart from God. It makes no difference whether you choose to say, "Oh, well, this is just a suggestion"; or, "This is hypnotism suggesting what appears to be a white poodle"; or, "This is a temptation to believe in a selfhood apart from God"; or whether you find other terms that you prefer, as long as you understand the essence of this truth and realize that you will never be called upon to heal a sick or sinning person because there is no such thing in the kingdom of God.

Right Identification and Reinterpretation

Never forget that this life of yours is God, and if it appears to you to be young or old, sick or well, evil or good, that is just God appearing to you, but incorrectly interpreted by you, and you are the one who must reinterpret the scene. There is no use going about saying, "Oh, I know there is no old age, sickness, or evil in heaven, but what about earth?" Heaven and earth are not two different places; heaven and earth are one and the same: Earth is our mortal concept of heaven, and heaven is our real awareness of the earth. In other words, heaven is the earth correctly understood.

Now follow this carefully. Here are two important points: right identification which means God appearing as individual life, the One appearing as many, or God, Life, appearing as individual being; and reinterpretation, which means looking at sick, sinning, dying humanity, and translating that appearance through the realization that, inasmuch as God is all, this is part of the allness of God which is being mis-seen, coming as a false suggestion, which must be reinterpreted.

These two important points you must carry with you from morning to night and night to morning—right identification and reinterpretation. Reinterpret everything you see, hear, taste, touch, and smell. Reinterpret it! Translate it into its original state which is Godhood. Practice right identification. Know that all that appears to you is God appearing—God appearing as individual man, woman, or child; God appearing as plant, animal, or crops.

What the human eye sees is the misconception of that divine idea. What the human eye sees or what the human ear hears is the false picture presented by this thing called hypnotism or suggestion, the same illusion that makes the tracks come together in the distance or the sky sit on the mountains. It makes no difference what name or term you use for error. Only be sure that you are not trying to be so absolute that you are unwilling to reinterpret what is appearing to you in the human scene.

For the serious student, the most important chapter in *The Infinite Way* is "The New Horizon,"[2] because in it can be found the explanation of the reinterpretation of what you behold. In other words, this chapter explains clearly that the entire human picture is mesmeric suggestion, and it is this suggestion of a selfhood apart from God that you are called upon to reinterpret.

After you have practiced this for awhile, it becomes automatic for you, as you see people and events, to translate or reinterpret them, and then you really see them as they are without any mental gyrations.

That is one reason so little treatment is needed in this work. The very moment a person, place, or condition presents itself to you, immediately should come the realization, "I know you! You are God appearing!" And if it is a sinful appearance, you can reinterpret it by remembering, "This is but a false sense of God appearing. This is suggestion, the human sense of things, and it is purely illusory." Thereby you learn not to fight or battle, but gradually to come into oneness with Reality.

The Consciousness of the Nothingness
of Error Must Be Gained

The nature of error has never been a pleasant subject to teach in metaphysics. Many truth-students do not like to hear about it. They would much rather spend their time talking about God and all the loveliness of God. I assure you that I, too, am one of those who would much rather adhere to the main theme of the Christ to the exclusion of this other aspect, but I have learned the danger of doing that. There are too many people in the metaphysical world who are perfectly willing to talk about the allness of God at the same moment that error is eating them up.

There are any number of people in the metaphysical world who are indulging in various forms of error. They justify themselves by saying, "Well, it hasn't any power"; yet they are indulging in it, so obviously it must have some power. Nevertheless, they look you right in the face and say, "Well, it has no power. What are you afraid of?" But at the same time that they are claiming it has no power and that they are not afraid of it, it still has enough power to attract them.

When you arrive at the place where you can look at every suggestion that presents itself to you and when you have reached such a high state of spiritual consciousness that every error coming to your attention drops away immediately, then you no longer need to take into consideration the nature of error. Most of us, however, have a long road to travel before that goal is reached.

As a matter of fact, probably most practitioners, that is, the spiritually enlightened ones, at some time or other, are so lifted up in consciousness that, when people come to them, the error drops away without their taking any conscious thought about it. Some of you have perhaps heard about the man with a visible growth who visited a practitioner during the 1933 Chicago World's Fair and asked her to talk to him about God. He did not ask for specific treatment, but she did as he asked—spent two hours talking about God. In the morning, the man's wife telephoned that the growth had entirely disappeared.

In those two hours, this practitioner had elevated herself to such a state of spiritual consciousness that she was no longer conscious of the condition that this man was presenting to her. In that purified state of consciousness, she did not have to declare, "This is suggestion!" because to her consciousness it was clearly evident that it was only suggestion.

It is not always necessary for you to make the statement, "Oh, this is suggestion!" or, "This is hypnotism and is not person, place, or thing!" I do not mean that at all. I do mean that it is necessary to arrive at that state of consciousness in which any form of error is instantly recognized as only suggestion and to stop giving treatments to people or conditions. Train yourself to know that you are never dealing with a sick or sinning person; you are never dealing with a disease: You are dealing only with universal beliefs.

My own grandfather was the victim of just such a universal belief. He became seriously ill when he was sixty-nine, and for awhile the family thought he would not survive, but he assured them, "Please do not be fearful of my passing on at this time. I am not going to die now because the Bible has promised me threescore years and ten and I am going to live until I reach that age." And he did!

Recognize the Nature of Error and Attain Mastery

The majority of people accept these universal beliefs at their face value, and then their life experience is influenced by them. We, however, must train ourselves not to accept world beliefs: Do not accept the suggestion of threescore years and ten; do not accept the suggestion that a disease is dangerous or serious. Remember, it is only suggestion.

Any belief can be set aside, but a law of God cannot be set aside. The law of God is life eternal. The law of God is: "All that I have is thine"—all the eternality, all the immortality. That cannot be set aside, but by becoming a law unto your own being through the realization that yours is a God-given dominion, the belief that you must die at any specific time can be set aside—whether it is a doctor who says it, whether it is the Bible with its threescore years and ten that says it, or whether it is the stars that say it. God gave man dominion over the things of the earth, over the waters, over the stars, over the heavens. God gave you, Its own individualized being, dominion, but you must consciously exercise this dominion and not sit back and let universal beliefs act upon you.

Remember that these beliefs, these universal beliefs—whether medical or theological—do act upon you until you consciously set them aside. In other words, every day of the year you are growing older, and unless you are consciously handling that belief and realizing, "My life is God, therefore ageless," you do come under this human belief about age and you will come to the place which is known as change of life, and eventually you will show forth signs of age, because you will pass through all the various phases of life in accordance with medical beliefs, until you yourself consciously take possession of your life through your God-given dominion and realize, "No! My life is God! Age and change are but medical beliefs or suggestions and do not have to operate in or upon or through my consciousness."

Thousands may fall at your left hand and tens of thousands at your right—if they do not take hold of this universal truth. Everyone has the right, either by choice or through ignorance, of going through life in his own way. You have the right to take hold of your own existence and determine its course and you do it in this way: When any form of error appears, be sure that you recognize it for what it is, so that it does not fool you. Do not let it cause you to accept a sick or sinful person and then try to reform or heal him. If you do that, you will be the blind leading the blind.

The only difference between a practitioner and a patient is that the practitioner cannot be hypnotized into believing that his patient is a human being. The practitioner knows that, regardless of appearances, his patient is God appearing as individual being, and the practitioner will not accept anything less than that. In the same way, the practitioner will not accept a sick person, a diseased person, or a sinning person as a patient. His response always is, "I know you! 'Get thee behind me, Satan!'[3] You are just a false sense tempting me into accepting you as reality. I know you, so you can take off your false face."

By reinterpretation and by right identification, you truly come into a state of consciousness in which life becomes, not a mental process, but a looking out and seeing God, seeing that all is well with the world.

~ 5 ~

MEDITATION

As one lives more and more in the Spirit, meditation[*] will undoubtedly play an increasingly important part in his life, because his periods of meditation are his point of contact with God.

The minute a person awakens in the morning and realizes, "I and my Father are one," he is meditating, he is going within and realizing the inner reality of being. Even if he declares this only once with his eyes closed, he has meditated on that particular idea. If he sits quietly, pondering, "Just as the wave is one with the ocean, just as a sunbeam is not something separate and apart from the sun, but really an emanation of the sun itself, so am I one with God," he is meditating.

There is nothing of a secret or occult nature about meditation—nothing strange or mysterious about the process, nor is there anything mysterious or hidden about the posture to be assumed in meditation. In fact, the only reason the subject of posture enters into a discussion of meditation at all is the common sense one of being comfortable.

Meditation is most easily achieved when the body is in such a position that it does not intrude into thought. In

---

[*]For a complete exposition of this subject, see the author's *The Art of Meditation*, ©1956 by Joel S. Goldsmith (New York: Harper & Row, paperback edition, 1990).

the Orient, few people ever sit on chairs, and therefore, sitting on the floor in a cross-legged position or with the feet underneath the body is natural for them. If I sit in a straight chair, with my feet planted firmly on the floor, my back straight as the backbone is supposed to be, and both hands resting in my lap—not resting on the chair where in a few minutes I might begin to feel the pressure of the wood, but in my lap—I am in a position where my body should not intrude itself into my thoughts. I should be able to maintain this position for five, six, ten, or twenty minutes without ever thinking about the body because that is a perfectly normal and natural position for those of the occidental world. The naturalness of the posture is primarily related to the customs prevalent in the country in which one happens to live.

Meditation is a practice which may extend over a period of five minutes or five hours, or be only a matter of seconds, so, therefore, I do not plan or think about any prescribed length of time I am going to meditate—whether five, twenty, or sixty minutes. The element of time is completely discounted, because if you think of the length of time, you may begin to think of the end of the period of meditation instead of leaving it alone and letting it work itself out. It may only be necessary for you to meditate two or three or four minutes. On the other hand, it may take six or seven or eight minutes for you to get that feeling of peace which marks the end of the meditation.

Contemplative meditation is nothing more nor less than pondering some idea of universal truth, which leads to the realization or conscious establishment of your unity with God. Therefore, do not take any of your problems into your meditation, but begin with some statement of truth which appeals to you or with some statement that you want to understand better, either a scriptural or a metaphysical statement, and see what happens.

Sitting in a normal and natural position, take the idea that "I and my Father are one." You may repeat that several times: "I and my Father are one. I and my Father are one." Then the thought may come: *"I*—if there is only one *I,* that *I* is God. I and the Father are one, and my being one with the Father makes all of the Father one with me, and it makes me one with all of the Father."

What you are doing is simply pondering this idea and its meaning because you do not want to form the undesirable habit of using any statement as a quotation. Just saying, "I and the Father are one," will not do a thing for you, but once that idea unfolds in your consciousness, once you have caught the import of the meaning of "I and my Father are one," you have achieved immortality, eternality, health, and wealth.

Disregard the Thoughts That Come in Meditation

Your meditation is really for the purpose of arriving at the real meaning, the inner meaning, of the statement, "I and my Father are one." As a beginner, however, you cannot keep that up for very long. You quickly lose the thread of it and find yourself thinking about whether you are missing your appointment at the office, or missing the bus or the train. The first thing you know, your thoughts are wandering.

At that point, gently bring your thought back to the statement, "I and my Father are one." Do not become impatient with yourself, do not condemn yourself, and do not think that you are hopeless. Pay no attention to this wandering of the mind, but gently bring your thought or attention back and begin again, pondering this idea, or possibly by that time some other idea will have come to you, probably a better one for the moment. As many times as your thought wanders from it, gently come back to the idea again, with no impatience, criticism, or judgment of yourself.

In this beginning state, it is not only that your thoughts wander, but your thoughts keep racing in and out—all kinds of undesirable thoughts. You may think they are your thoughts. They are not. They are just banging away at you, trying to disturb and distract you, so do not fight them, do not try to stop thinking these thoughts, because you cannot succeed, and knowing that, may save you a great deal of trouble. You will never succeed in stopping your thinking, so let those thoughts come in and go out and do anything they want to do. Do not be concerned about them. Just hew to your center, to the particular subject of your meditation.

There will come a time as you continue in this practice when extraneous thoughts will not come, because you will have starved them by neglect; you will have made yourself so unreceptive to them by not fighting them that they will not return. If you fight them, however, they will be there forever because your fighting them is the very thing that keeps them alive. "Agree with thine adversary quickly, whiles thou art in the way with him."[1] All these wrong thoughts that keep recurring are not dangerous or harmful; nobody will know about them; and they will not hurt you. Let them come; let them go; but pay no attention to them.

Always remember that you are in meditation but for one purpose—to realize God. And so you ponder on these scriptural truths: "I and my Father are one.[2]. . . My kingdom is not of this world. . . .[3] Thou wilt keep him in perfect peace, whose mind is stayed on thee."[4] Choose one of your own, or you may reach the point where something you need for that particular day will come to you, and you will ponder that.

The point I am making is that you take some central thought or inspiring quotation into meditation, not for the purpose of repeating it, but for the purpose of discovering its real or inner meaning, so that you never again use it or even think of it as a quotation.

I can remember for how many months I lived with the statement, "Not by might, nor by power, but by my spirit."[5] Finally I arrived at the place where it spoke to me in these words, "Not by *physical* might, nor by *mental* power, but by *My Spirit*—by the reality of my own being." I practiced this for eight months, five, six, and eight times a day, before I arrived at the place of even one second of peace and quiet within.

But you will never have to go through the various stages of somebody else's development. You will never have to drive Model T Fords. You will never have to light your house with kerosene lamps. You will not have to go through those trying days of giving mental treatments and worrying about what evil influences are coming to bear upon you. You can begin with the highest point of development which has been reached up to this time; you can begin at the highest level that has been revealed to consciousness, because all the people who have gone through those things have paved the way for you.

So with meditation. You will find before long that original ideas or quotations will come to you—I use "original" in the sense that these have not been given to you by any person, but that they have come directly to you—and that you are able to settle down for a minute, or two or three or four, of peace.

Meditation Is a State of Receptivity and Alertness

As you are pondering some quotation and utterly disregarding the human thoughts that come and go, do one more thing: Keep your ear alert as if you were going to hear something. This is not because you actually may hear anything in meditation or that you necessarily must hear anything. It is only that the ear is the finite concept of hearing and it represents to us "the listening ear."

The listening ear is not a physical instrument in any sense of the word. Jesus said, "Having eyes, see ye not? and having ears, hear ye not?"[6] That statement has nothing to do with a physical eye, nor with a physical ear. Therefore, when I speak of keeping this "ear" open, it makes no difference whether or not a voice is heard. This is just a human concept of the spiritual idea of receptivity.

Thus, while meditating on some particular idea, you are keeping your ear open, alert and receptive, because meditation has nothing to do with resting or falling asleep. On the contrary, it is the keenest state of alertness. A person who knows how to meditate will never fall asleep. As a matter of fact, two, three, or four minutes of meditation are enough to drive away all the tiredness one may feel after a whole day's work. Meditation is letting in the divine Spirit, God, and that dispels every illusion of sense.

One of the reasons I advise students not to place a time limit on meditation is because meditation must never become a mental effort. The very minute that it begins to be a bore or an effort, it should be stopped. Never let it become an effort. Do not strain. You are not going to get into the kingdom of God by force; you are never going to take heaven by any mental or physical power. If your meditation has been of only one and one-half minutes' duration, be satisfied, because if you have been holding to the idea of God for but half a minute, you have been opening your consciousness—you have started the inflow. You may not get an answer at that moment, although you may get one twelve hours later or possibly twelve days later, but the important thing is that you have opened consciousness to the inflow of truth.

To begin with, meditate three times a day, or least twice—morning and night. There is nobody who cannot do that because everybody gets up and everybody goes to bed, so everybody can spare an extra couple of minutes in the morning and an extra couple of minutes at night, even if no other minute during the day can be found. As you continue this practice, some of you will find that, between getting up in the morning and going to bed at night, there is another interval of two or three minutes to give to meditation.

So, to begin with, if you will give two or three or four minutes, two or three times a day, to this little process, it will of itself stretch out into longer periods. And then what follows is up to the individual. You may arrive at that place where you can sit in meditation for four hours and at the end of that length of time really feel, "My, these ten minutes flew by in a hurry!" That is an individual experience. There are people who will never achieve that because they are not temperamentally suited to it, but everyone can achieve meditation in some degree, if only for three, four, or five minutes.

After this becomes an almost regular part of your daily routine, gradually, you are going to find that you can meditate at any hour of the day or night—sometimes for half a second and sometimes for minutes on end, even while driving your car, doing housework, or sitting and talking to a person.

You can learn to open your consciousness for just that second and find yourself in a state of receptivity, and once that line is open, once you have become a state of receptivity, your guidance, leading, direction, and help flow continuously through you. It is as if you had opened up a line to God, and from that moment on, it just pours through and appears as you need it. If you need direction, it says to you, "Don't go this way," or, "Go this way." If you need money, it appears; if you need a parking space, it appears—but not because you are demonstrating *things.*

For example, there could be no Niagara Falls without a Lake Erie. Or shall we put it another way? You cannot demonstrate Niagara Falls, but by having the consciousness of a Lake Erie there can be a Niagara Falls, but it would be senseless to go about trying to demonstrate a Niagara Falls separate and apart from Lake Erie. Once you have a Lake Erie, you have a Niagara Falls on the American side and one on the Canadian side too, but you must be sure that you have the consciousness of Lake Erie, and then Niagara Falls automatically follows.

Living by the Word

Never violate the commandment, "Seek ye first the kingdom of God, and his righteousness; and all these things shall be added unto you."[7] Meditation is not a method of acquiring things, but an at-one-ment with the divine source of Being.

Let me explain it this way. As human beings we seem to be so many feet tall and so many pounds heavy. We live by bread: the food we eat, the water we drink, the air we breathe—these really constitute us as human beings. But if we are to live the spiritual life, we are told not to live by bread alone. What then do we live by? "By every word that proceedeth out of the mouth of God"[8]— not by quotations, not by affirmations or denials, but by every idea of intelligence and love, by every activity of consciousness. That is what we live by.

As human beings we do not have the Word. It is only when we have opened ourselves to this contact with the infinity of Being—with the ocean of Knowledge, the ocean of Love—that divine inspiration flows, the wine of which Jesus spoke, the water, and the bread. From that moment on we do not live "by bread alone." Oh yes, we live by bread, and cake, too; but we are not living by bread alone.

Do you remember how the people told Jesus that Moses had given their fathers "bread from heaven to eat,"[9] but that Jesus replied, "Moses gave you not that bread from heaven; but my Father giveth you the true bread from heaven. For the bread of God is he which cometh down from heaven, and giveth life unto the world. . . . I am the bread of life: he that cometh to me shall never hunger; and he that believeth on me shall never thirst."[10] The bread that Moses gave was bread for their hunger, but if you eat of the spiritual bread, you will never hunger, and for water you will never thirst.

Moses gave them water, too—water which he made come out of the rocks. But that was not the spiritual water: That was only improved humanhood. That was just as if I would sit here and demonstrate another twenty-five or fifty dollars a week's income for you. It would be like Moses' demonstration of increased good. But if I can show you how to open your consciousness to the inflow of God, then whatever of increased good comes to you, is not an increase of humanhood: It is the Divine, Itself, and Its flow never stops. That is why you will never hunger once that bread comes to you.

I remember when I first went into the healing work, I followed the procedure of most of the practitioners I knew, entering all absent treatments, present treatments, and office treatments in a book; and then at the end of the month, I meticulously tabulated all of these and sent out bills on the bill-heads which I had had printed. That went on until the realization came that this was not living from God—this was living from the Smiths and Browns who were paying me their bills. And what would happen to me if they did not pay? That was a poser, for then I would be in a predicament. From that time on I stopped all that. I began to realize that if I could demonstrate that by the love of God alone, my bills were paid in any one month, I would be safe for life. The love of God could never be taken away from me, and that flow could never be stopped once it had been contacted.

That is the secret. Once you touch this Christ, once you touch this center of Consciousness, once you open your consciousness to the inflow of the health of God, of spiritual supply, you will never again hunger; you will never have demonstrations of supply to make. In family relationships, too, once you have touched the idea of the love that comes from God, you will find it in wife, husband, or child.

It is through meditation that this contact is made, and that is why meditation is so important—not merely a sitting down for a few moments, for I know the day will come when you will be driving your car and meditating, you will be sleeping at night and meditating, because you will be sleeping in God-consciousness instead of the comatose brain.

In meditation you will receive ideas of truth, ideas which exteriorize themselves in what is recognized as tangible form, as bread on the table, as healing, or as truth that dispels error. Meditation even reveals the true nature of error as the illusion which it is. Only do not try to exert mental effort. It is "not by might, nor by power"—it is by the gentle Spirit.

~ 6 ~

TEACHING THE MESSAGE

For the benefit of those who are having patients or students coming to them and who are not only trying to bring about healing for them, but at the same time introduce them to the subject of spiritual truth, let me point out that one of the first things that must be taught to the person who either has had little or no experience in metaphysics or to the one who is coming from some other school of metaphysics into the Infinite Way is the meaning of terms like Soul, Consciousness, and the Christ.

Rarely do you meet a lay person in this work—I don't mean practitioners, I mean an average patient or student—who has caught the vision of the word, "Soul." It is one of the most misunderstood words in metaphysics and is so important that, without an understanding of it, the spiritual vision of this message cannot be perceived.

The Soul-Faculties and Consciousness

Soul, or Consciousness, is the seat of those faculties which we interpret as physical organs and functions and physical faculties or physical senses. The day will come when, if you know enough about Consciousness, you can leave everything else alone, for in the word, "Consciousness," and the spiritual understanding of it, is contained all the knowledge that is to be known about God, man, and the universe. As a matter of fact, the five senses—sight, hearing, taste, touch, and smell—sometimes metaphysically called "the unreal senses," are but our misinterpretation of Consciousness.

For example, if I see you, I am conscious of your presence through the faculty of sight; if I hear you, I am conscious of your presence through the organs of hearing; and, of course, I can also become conscious of you through my sense of smell or taste. But what is happening is that I am conscious of you. Therefore, the five senses are really just five different facets of the activity of Consciousness, which is the one real faculty and is spiritual; they are but the finite sense of that one spiritual activity, Consciousness.

Inasmuch as we do not deny the body and do not deny the senses, we have to account for them; and as has been previously explained, it is through right identification and reinterpretation that we find we really have these activities of Consciousness which are called sight, hearing, taste, touch, and smell—only instead of five, there are seven.

There is the faculty of intuition, and there is also the faculty of Consciousness which is without any thought process or any outer process—it is actually a silence. In that silence, which is the ultimate, we are alive in God, experiencing only God acting through, or as, individual you and me.

However, the activity of Consciousness can be called the Soul-sense, in contradistinction to the five physical senses. Without eyes, it is possible to see, and this I have done repeatedly and can do at will through inner vision, but this inner vision involves the development of the

Soul-sense. For example, years ago in experimenting with the development of that sense, I found that the time came when I could be in a dark room in the country at midnight, with no lights at all, blindfold myself, and in a few minutes I could see every detail of the room and see even outside the room. That was because consciousness was operating without the limitation of physical eyes.

Seeing without eyes is similar to hearing "the still small voice" which is just another facet of the same thing. If you skeptically doubt or deny the possibility of such an experience, the next time you hear "the still small voice" you will have to deny that too, because you are hearing without ears, that is, without using the organs of hearing.

I know that this is possible because of the experience of a member of my family, who was a musician and who through an illness became stone deaf. It was discovered upon examination that both eardrums were broken, and he was told that never again would he hear. One of his relatives who was just becoming interested in spiritual healing asked him to have treatments, and because of this insistence he had one treatment, and from that day to this his hearing has been perfect—but he still has no eardrums. Because of his work—he is no longer a musician but an engineer—he has been required to have many physical examinations, especially during the war. Each time the physician has declared that it is impossible for him to hear—but he does, and without any hearing aid. Undoubtedly, the practitioner who opened up the Soul-sense of hearing for him must have reached an exceptionally high state of consciousness to bring about such a healing.

Life as Consciousness

Another example of life as Consciousness is that of Brown Landone who, in 1931 at the age of about eighty years, collapsed in The Pennsylvania Hotel in New York City. Physicians who were called in while he was still unconscious stated that he could not live more than two hours. When x-rays were taken, the verdict was that no one could possibly live even minutes, certainly not over two hours, with a heart in the condition his was.

When Mr. Landone became conscious, he was told that he had but a short time left and that he should get his affairs in order, if he could, as quickly as possible. To this he replied, "If I have only two hours, I am going to spend them at my desk finishing important work."

With that he got up, and the next day he was still at his desk, working. Several times the doctors came in to examine him, and each time they said it was a miracle, but certainly he could not go on for another two hours. In spite of their prognosis, however, he lived and continued to work for about twenty years more, never again knowing a sick moment. His was a case of a man who lived and worked without what is known as a normal heart.

He had reached the place where he knew that God is life and that God-life has nothing to do with what is called physical form. When Brown Landone left this experience, it was neither through disease nor accident, but only because he felt the time had come and that he was called to do some other work. He turned to his secretary and said, "I am leaving you"; and without ever having had even a sick moment, sat down and left. He was then ninety-seven years of age, plus.

These things are possible if, in your consciousness, life has been lifted above the physical plane, but do not think for a minute that a practitioner can give a treatment and have a person hear without ears or live without a heart. No practitioner can do that any more than can a doctor. But if the practitioner catches this glimpse of life as God, then there is no longer any living in a body or through a body. The body then is merely the vehicle. Life is within, or as, consciousness, and that is completely independent of physicality.

If you have no inclination to accept the two above mentioned experiences as possible, or if you are the kind of person who believes only what you can become aware of with your physical senses, that is, if you deny the validity of spiritual experiences, then you must accept the theory that life and consciousness end with the grave, because if consciousness and life cannot go on separate and apart from what is known as physical form, then of course there is extinction at the grave. What you wish to believe is up to you. You can take your choice, but unless you can accept what I am telling you, your belief in immortality is going to be badly shaken.

The Christ

To the average metaphysician, the Christ still is an unknown factor. Most people think of the Christ more as a person than as what It really is. The Christ really and truly is one's individual identity, one's real being. The Christ is individual consciousness when it has been purged of all love, fear, or hate of error of any nature. When you no longer love, fear, or hate error in any form, you are Christ-consciousness. Too many believe that Christ, or Christ-consciousness, is something separate and apart from their own being—something that is not an integral part of their being, but which may perhaps be attained.

As a matter of fact, Christ-consciousness can be attained, but it can be attained only in one way, that is, through our recognition of the nature of error which causes us to lose our love, our hate, or our fear of it. Just as we have to arrive at an understanding of God appearing as man, so we also have to realize Christ as immanent, as the Christ of our own being, the Christ of our own consciousness. Otherwise, there will be a patient or student *and* a God separate and apart, or a patient or student separate and apart from the Christ.

The Difference Between Prayer and Treatment

Another important aspect of the Infinite Way which students should be led to understand is the difference between prayer and treatment. In *Spiritual Interpretation of Scripture,* it has been made clear that these are not synonymous: Treatment consists of statements of truth which we may make for the purpose of reminding ourselves of the truth of being and for the purpose of gaining a conscious realization of the truth of being, either through the spoken word or through meditation or cogitation. Prayer, on the other hand, only begins when we have finished with thinking, with making statements or reviewing thoughts or ideas.

Prayer is that which takes place when we have come to the end of the treatment and sit with that listening ear and receive impartations, receive a message or a feeling, an awareness from within. Prayer is the word of God, but He speaks it to our individual consciousness, or within our individual consciousness. Therefore, those who have developed the listening ear, the attitude of receptivity, are those who receive the word of God, called prayer, and that results in healing and regeneration—in any change necessary in the outer picture.

Improvement Comes Through the Introduction of the Christ into Consciousness

Remember that there is no change in the outer scene until there is a change in our state of consciousness, and what change can there be unless something higher enters to change us? And where does that come from? Our thinking mind? No, we have to resort to something higher than the thinking mind.

Humanhood will not improve humanhood. Something higher is necessary, because it is only through spiritual sense, or the Christ, that a person can be improved. Even if you could make a person a better human being, you would have done nothing toward spiritualizing him. Never forget this. A better human being is a better human being, no more, no less: He is not spiritual consciousness.

Therefore, if you tell a person, "Oh, if you only had a better disposition! If you could just overcome impatience, then you would get a healing! If you would just get rid of jealousy, if you would only get rid of hate!" he might well reply, "Yes, I'd just love to get rid of all those things, but how can I?" Tell me, how does a person overcome jealousy, hatred, and impatience, or get rid of intolerance or injustice? How does he become more grateful? He doesn't, if he is looking to his humanhood to do it for him because if that were possible, he would have done it long ago.

There is no way humanly to overcome undesirable personal characteristics, except by will power; and when you do that you risk damming them up in one place only to have them break out again in a worse form at another time, in another place. Only the introduction of the Christ into individual consciousness will destroy jealousy, hate, enmity, injustice, dishonesty, immorality, and sensuality. Sometimes this is accomplished through the reading of metaphysical literature or scriptural writings. Sometimes just one statement registers in a person's consciousness, and it makes him a new man. Sometimes, as was my experience in 1928, it may be brought about through meeting an individual of such high consciousness that when his consciousness touches yours your whole human past is wiped out—that part of it that you wanted wiped out or which needed to be wiped out.

Over and over it happens that when people come to a practitioner who is in a high spiritual state or is normally of high spiritual consciousness, automatically they feel their fears drop away, or they feel their antagonism, or their hate, enmity, dishonesty, or sensuality just fade away. That is because they have been touched by the Christ of the person known as a practitioner, teacher, or lecturer.

An individual can do this for himself sometimes merely through the reading of spiritual literature which either suddenly or gradually brings about a change in his entire nature because it is introducing the Christ into human consciousness. Any way in which an individual is brought into the conscious presence of the Christ serves as an avenue through which that human improvement takes place.

Our first work with the young student is bringing to light the truth that God is the mind of the individual; God is the life, the Soul, and the Spirit, even the substance of the body of the person appearing for the moment as patient or student. In other words, in our work the main point is that there is not God *and* man. Probably this approach is unique in that. You cannot give a treatment to man because in this approach man is not separate and apart from God, but God appears as man.

So it would be an impossibility for a practitioner to give a treatment to a man, woman, or child if he understood clearly that all that is appearing as man, woman, or child is God, the one Life, the one Soul and Spirit, and that even the body of that individual is the temple of the living God, and the mind Its instrument.

Spiritual Integrity Is Vital

The subject of error should be very lightly touched upon with the young student and not dealt with in its deeper aspects until he is well prepared for it. It is not an easy subject and certainly cannot be taught to anyone until the practitioner or teacher himself has really mastered it.

Spiritual teaching is not the transfer of thought from one individual to another. It is the impartation of consciousness from God, and in that lifting up of consciousness, all necessary knowledge is received.

The teacher must be careful never to pass on to a patient or a student quotations or statements, which might be considered in the nature of clichés, until he has at least demonstrated the truth of them in some degree. There is nothing worse in this work than hollow phrases and statements. In their enthusiasm, many practitioners are likely to retort glibly to any call made upon them, "Oh, you know it isn't real!" Of course a person asking for help doesn't know it isn't real, and, moreover, had the practitioner known that whatever he was talking about was not real, the patient would have been healed in that moment, and he would never have had to voice it.

Most of us make too many biblical or metaphysical statements to our patients and students, many of which we ourselves have not mastered. True, the authority for our statements may be Jesus or some metaphysical teacher or writer, but even so, before we quote them, we ourselves should have some understanding of them. Then these statements come forth from our own consciousness, and our patient or student understands and accepts them readily. Otherwise, they are very likely to reject any statement we make which we have not in a measure demonstrated.

It was Emerson who said, "What you are . . . thunders so that I cannot hear what you say." And that is the truth about us. What we are within our own being is so much a part of our consciousness that if we attempt to voice anything not fully a part of us, nobody will believe us.

Suppose I declare as a spiritual truth, "There is only one Self; there is only one life," and yet, when some occasion arises, I lie or cheat a little. To whom am I lying and whom am I cheating, since there is only one Self? Whom am I deceiving, since there is only one mind and one life?

A good human being might go through life without ever cheating anyone of a single nickel, but that would not be spiritual integrity. That would be just human goodness. Spiritual integrity is living up to one's understanding of spiritual truth and living the Christ-ideal. That does not mean merely living a good human life or being a good moral person. Human good is not what I mean by spiritual integrity, because one could be humanly perfect and not measure up to the standard of spiritual integrity.

Spiritual integrity is the realization of the one Self as the Self of me and the Self of all men, of the one mind and the one life as the mind and life of me and of all men; and therefore, the interests of one are the interests of all. That is living up to spiritual integrity because that is making thought and action conform to our understanding of oneness.

Suppose I accept spiritually the teaching that all that the Father has is mine, and then I envy somebody his possessions. I am then violating my own spiritual integrity. I am not injuring the person I envy; he is not affected by it at all; but I am violating my own conviction that all that the Father has is mine because I am not acting on my own conviction. I am double-minded. I am saying in one breath, "Life is one," but at the same time I am setting up two—myself and the person I am envying, cheating, or defrauding.

In other words, spiritual integrity means living according to the Sermon on the Mount, "Whatsoever ye would that men should do to you, do ye even so to them."[1] But the reason for living the Sermon on the Mount is not for the sake of being a good human being, but because you realize that the other Self is you, and you are the other Self.

If you maintain this oneness in your consciousness continuously, living out from it, you are maintaining your spiritual integrity. If you never said a word to anyone, if you never preached a sermon on honesty, integrity, or loyalty, all those touching your consciousness would sense those qualities emanating from you because that is your state of consciousness, that is what you are.

Never indulge thoughts or acts that violate the teaching of the one Self. What about criticizing, judging, and condemning another person? When you do that, you are only doing it to yourself, and it is bound to come back to you. Do not ever believe that your own errors will not come back to you. They will. In judging or condemning anyone or anything, you are violating your own understanding that there is only One and are in reality judging and condemning your own being.

When you accept the spiritual teaching of oneness—of the one Self, of the one mind, as the mind of every individual, of one Life, one Soul, one Spirit—and live it, you can see that you will be helping to usher in the millennium, bringing about the time when no one could possibly act or think or do to another that which he would not do to his own being, because he would know that the Self of the other person is the Self of his own being.

Ordination

Two statements from the Master I give you: "My kingdom is not of this world. . ."[2] and "I have overcome the world."[3]

Three men who are known to have had their own revelation of the complete secret of life are Lao-tze of China, about 600 B.C.; Buddha of India, about 550 B.C.; and Jesus of Nazareth. Through Jesus, the full revelation came to the beloved disciple, John, on the Isle of Patmos.

It was through Jesus that I, too, received this same unfoldment through his statement in the Bible, "My kingdom is not of this world," and this statement together with, "I have overcome the world," became the subject of my meditation for many months. I did not choose them; they clung to me, and finally came the realization of their meaning. I have never known this to be taught since it was received by John, except in his own veiled writings, and so if you can receive and accept this teaching, God has indeed blessed you beyond all men and women.

To overcome the world means to overcome, or rise above, all sense desire, to be free of world attraction, to live in the world but be not of it, to attain freedom from bondage to personal ego, and to understand the spiritual world and thus gain freedom from the false sense of God's universe. As we humanly see this world, we are seeing God's heaven, but seeing it "through a glass, darkly."[4] To overcome this world means to rise above the human, finite, erroneous sense of the world, and see it as it is.

It was John who told us, "When he shall appear, we shall be like him; for we shall see him as he is."[5] In this enlightened consciousness, we shall see God face to face, even though it is God appearing as you or as me, God appearing as individual man or woman.

These words clearly show forth the higher consciousness of life, but only as you can be reached within and open your consciousness spiritually can you come into the actual awareness of them. This is spiritual baptism, the Pentecostal experience of receiving the Holy Ghost. From it you will emerge as men and women who have seen through the mirage of sense testimony to the underlying reality in which you actually live and move and have your being.

This life you live is God seen "through a glass, darkly," but now, in this instant, face to face. You can now enjoy friendships, companionships, marriage, business associations, but all without intense attachment. The great successes of your friends or families will not unduly elate you, and their failures will not too greatly disturb you.

You will use dollars as a medium of exchange, but never again will you, who overcome this world, hate or fear or love them. You will handle dollars as you handle streetcar transfers—necessary and desirable paraphernalia of daily experience. You will always possess more than you need, without taking any anxious thought. Even the temporary absence of dollars will not embarrass or trouble you because nothing in your world is dependent upon them. All that you require comes to you through grace and as the gift of God.

In overcoming this world, you overcome the beliefs which constitute this world, including the belief that man must earn his living by the sweat of his brow. You are joint-heir with Christ in God to all the heavenly riches, to every idea of infinite Wisdom.

In overcoming this world, you lose your fear of the body, thereby freeing it to live under God's law. You overcome the world's beliefs about the body—that it is finite or material, that it lives by bread alone or by so-called material foods, or that it must be catered to in any way. Bathe it, keep it clean, inside and out, but drop all concern for it. It is in God's eternal keeping. It is living and moving and having its being in God-consciousness. Take no thought for your body, for it is God's concern to preserve and maintain the immortality of His own universe, including His body, which is the only body.

What you physically see as your body represents your concept of body, but there is only one body, the body of God, and this is the secret of secrets.

God's health is your health. God's wealth is your wealth.

Your family is the household of God, your consciousness of God's infinite, individual being. There is only one Being, and that One is God, and every person you meet represents your concept of that One, individually expressed.

Your spiritual freedom means your freedom from the false and universal beliefs about your body, your affairs, and your relationships. You are then no longer under the law of universal belief: You are set free in Christ, that is, you have overcome or risen above the erroneous beliefs about God's world, and therefore, you have overcome this world, the false sense of the world. You now see the world as it really is and not as "this world."

"My peace I give unto you: not as the world giveth." [6] *Spiritual peace I give you, the peace that passeth understanding, the peace that is not dependent upon person or outer condition. Now, nothing in this world can affect you who are free in Christ, in spiritual consciousness. You will walk up and down the world, come and go freely, and none of the world beliefs will kindle upon you. The flames will not harm you; the waters will not drown. I have put My seal upon you, and you are free. Walk up and down, in and out. Spiritual law upholds your being, your body, your business.*

Tell no man what things you have seen and heard. Do not explain or tell people of your freedom from "this world." Move in and out among men, as a blessing, as a benediction, as the light of the world. Let this life and mind be in you which was in Christ Jesus. Be receptive. Be expectant. Be always alert to receive inner guidance and direction and support. Keep attuned to your world within, yet fulfill all your duties without. Fulfill all your obligations without, but keep alert within.

There are those of you who have been called to God's work. It will be given you what to do and when. I have put My Spirit upon you. This Spirit will be seen and felt by men. It will not be you, but the Spirit they will discern, although they will think of It as you.

*My Spirit will work for you and with you and through you and as you. It will work to accomplish My purpose. You will be My presence on earth. I will not leave you, nor forsake you. In any appearance I will still be with you. Fear nothing of this world. My guiding Spirit is ever with you.**

Of Lao-tze it is said that when he was 1200 years old he grew weary because the world could not accept freedom from the grind of mortal living. He decided to leave the city, but before going through the gate, the gatekeeper, suspecting that he would never return, asked him to write down his teaching, which he did in a short message. Then he went out into the wilds of China and was never again seen.

Of Buddha, it is said that he taught his disciples, but found they could not fully realize the import of the message, so one day he sent for them, bade them farewell, and left this human plane.

Jesus asked, "Could ye not watch with me one hour?"[7] He also said, "If I go not away, the Comforter [the spirit

---

*The italicized passages of this book are spontaneous meditations that have come to the author during periods of uplifted consciousness and are not in any sense intended to be used as affirmations, denials, or formulas. They have been inserted in this book from time to time to serve as examples of the free flowing of the Spirit.

of Truth] will not come unto you."[8]—meaning that even the disciples had not grasped the significance of his message.

Again, now, the Message is repeated on earth to you. Will you also sleep?

~7~

MAKING THE ADJUSTMENT

The readers of this book naturally represent varying states and stages of consciousness. Some may be widely experienced in metaphysical work from the standpoint of Christian Science or Unity, some from the standpoint of other metaphysical approaches, and others may be practically beginners and know nothing about the spiritual approach to life.

Therefore, it is difficult to reach these different thought patterns and expect all of them to understand the same things in the same way. For that reason, this chapter is devoted to bringing about an understanding of the language used in the Infinite Way. While I do not claim that the truth expressed in the Infinite Way has not at some time or other been included in the teachings of the great sages and seers, it must be recognized that this particular approach–the particular meaning of the truth or the purpose of this teaching–is probably different from almost any other teaching.

The Infinite Way stands wholly and completely on the revelation of Jesus as given in the Gospel according to John. There is no deviation from Jesus' teaching in one single particle, nor are we, in explaining or elucidating it, adding to it or taking from it in any way. It is accepted absolutely as it stands in the revelation of Jesus: I *am life eternal;* I *am the way, the truth, and the light.* I *am the resurrection—not, I will be resurrected, not that there is some kind of a law of God which is going to act upon me, but I am the resurrection. I am the bread—not, I will be supplied with bread, but I am the bread; I am the water; I am the wine.*

When you stand on that, you stand on the revelation that you are infinite spiritual consciousness, infinite spiritual life itself, and being infinite, all inclusive and including within your own being every activity of Being.

God Appears as Individual Being

Those of you who are familiar with metaphysical teachings must realize that the Infinite Way is in contra-distinction to most of the current metaphysical movements. It teaches that no one can help you demonstrate anything. In this teaching, you must realize the infinite nature of your own being, and let all *things* be added unto you. This sets up for you an entirely new and different approach to life. It takes you out of the realm of being an idea, a reflection, an expression, or an image, and of having to demonstrate something from the Father.

So in that way alone, this is a radical departure, because you are working from the standpoint: *I and the Father are one. Therefore, I include all that the Father has and all that the Father is.* And so you commit a sin every time you allow your thought to go out into the realm of "I desire," "I want," or, "I fear."

I and the Father are one, and all that the Father has is mine. I include all the qualities and activities of the Godhead. I am the very embodiment of all that the Father is, not because I deserve it, but because it is mine by grace: It is the gift of God to God's own creation.

As a matter of fact, it is cheering to know that even God cannot take any good away from us. God is all power, but not that powerful! He cannot take our good away from us, because He would be taking it away from His own Self. We are not two: We are one!

If any one of us were to be deprived of a single bit of good on earth, God would be depriving Himself. That is obviously impossible. "I and my Father are one.[1] . . . Son, thou art ever with me, and all that I have is thine,"[2] not by virtue of any human goodness, but by divine right.

> The Spirit itself beareth witness with our spirit, that we are the children of God: And if children, then heirs; heirs of God, and joint-heirs with Christ.
>
> Romans 8:16, 17

> Lo, I am with you alway, even unto the end of the world.
>
> Matthew 28:20

> Fear not: for I have redeemed thee, I have called thee by thy name; thou art mine. When thou passest through the waters, I will be with thee; and through the rivers, they shall not overflow thee: when thou walkest through the fire, thou shalt not be burned; neither shall the flame kindle upon thee.
>
> Isaiah 43:1, 2

Those are all divine promises, but being a good human being will not bring us these spiritual blessings, although the realization of the spiritual blessing always bestowed on the beloved son of God will make of us good human beings. All the human good we can do in the world will not earn for us one single bit of God's grace, but God's grace will make of you and of me the finest kind of human beings in the world. That is the mystery of godliness.

"Take No Thought"

The approach of the Infinite Way is very radical, also, in its following of the teaching of the Master:

"Take no thought for your life, what ye shall eat, or what ye shall drink; nor yet for your body, what ye shall put on."[3] We must come into this realization: "My heavenly Father, which is my own infinite consciousness, knoweth what things I have need of, and it is His good pleasure to give me the kingdom."

You must understand that this teaching is not meant to give you a method by which to demonstrate better or longer humanhood, nor is it a teaching of how to use your mind to get things or to do things for you, or to give you some power called God to bring you human things or human betterment.

This is a teaching which is meant to take you out of humanhood into the awareness of your spiritual identity. This is a way of life which teaches you how to be in the world, but not of it; it is a way of life which teaches that from the beginning of time, since before Abraham was, *I Am,* and that *I* will be right here until the end of the world.

Therefore, the purpose of this teaching is to build a state of consciousness in which you never take thought for a person, place, or thing in this world, and yet find yourself moving in and among and with and through persons and places and things—"in green pastures . . . beside the still waters."[4] Conscious thinking does not do this; treatment does not do this: The law of God which you are in your innermost being is what does it, and your only part is to be grateful for all the loving, kind, and generous people with whom you come in contact, for all the beauty you are permitted to see, and for all the joyous experiences that come to you.

This is developing a state of consciousness which is that of a beholder, a witness to God's work. That is all. You are a spectator watching the divine Play, watching the divine flow of Life, through you, in you, and as you. You live and move and have your being in God. This power of Good acts upon you—not really upon you, but *as* you. You are It in action.

"I have overcome the world."[5] How can anyone make the statement, "I have overcome the world," as long as he has any anxiety about anything there is between the bottom of the ocean and the top of the stars. You cannot say, " 'I have overcome the world,' but I am afraid of a bullet or an atomic bomb!" You cannot even say that you have overcome the world if you fear or believe that death is a possibility or an inevitability or that you will be any different from what you are this minute, after you have experienced what the world calls death.

"I have overcome the world" means that the belief of separation, of lack and limitation, of sin and disease, of desire, of fear, envy, hate, jealousy, and malice has been overcome. To you, that may seem like the millennium. And it is—so far as you and I are concerned. For us, it is the millennium because we have approached that place where death does not exist any more as a reality, where lack and limitation, where sin and fear do not exist any more.

In making a transition of such magnitude, it is natural that there will be an overturning in thought, a certain amount of questioning, for the simple reason that you are being roused out of your humanhood. This teaching, if it does nothing else, will lift you forcibly out of a great degree of humanhood. It certainly will not leave you where it found you! Either you will notice that you have been roused out of a lethargy, or you will find yourself freed from the pressure arising out of attempts to demonstrate by mental means, or released from the compulsion of having to demonstrate health, supply, this, that, or the other thing every day of the year. All of a sudden you find that your mind is no longer being used for any such purpose. This, in itself, is disturbing.

It is really an upsetting experience to stop thinking, sit back, and just rest in God. At first it makes you afraid, and you wonder if you will wake up tomorrow if you do not read your "daily lesson." In this work I have known people who gave up doing "the daily lesson" and others who felt impelled to give up their affirmations and denials, and I have observed how some of them marveled that the sky did not collapse and fall down upon them for failing to go through these routines and rituals. It did not, and it will not! There is a God.

There is a God, but you know right well that not too many of us believe it. We have believed that our affirmations and denials or our treatment was the God that made everything all right. And that is not God at all. *I Am* is God—and every time you say, "I am," you are declaring the presence and the power of God in your experience.

You could go through the remainder of your life without a treatment, without a lesson, or without reading a book, and find greater harmonies, greater peace, and greater health than you have ever known—just through the simple realization of "Thank You, Father; I am." That is enough. That is the acknowledgment of Deity; it is the acknowledgment of an infinite invisible Presence and Power which is the reality of your own being. That is all anybody ever needs. All the books that you read, all the notes that you take, all the talks and lectures you attend, and all your meditations—all these have but the one purpose of bringing you to the conscious realization: "I already am."

Strange, is it not? All these years and only now are we waking up to the fact that *I already am.* Your reading will not establish God. Your reading will not make error any less error than the nothingness it already is. Your reading and your meditations are only for the purpose of coming into the realization that that which has been since before Abraham, and is now and ever will be, really and truly is your life.

Demonstrability and Practicability, the Authority

Inevitably the question arises, "Who and what is the authority for such a statement?" Such a question can be answered by turning to the teachings of the Master, Christ Jesus, as recorded in the New Testament, but the authority for any teaching is in its results, in what it has accomplished and what it is accomplishing for those who live by it. In other words, the proof of the pudding is in the eating—not in who originated the recipe.

Even though Jesus did give this truth to the world, he certainly was not the originator of it. Throughout his whole human history he gave credit to the Hebrew prophets and the law makers. Those who study comparative religion or the many and diverse philosophies of the world, which antedate Jesus by thousands of years, will find every statement that Jesus made in much the same form, or, if in other forms, with practically the same essence.

So it is not necessary to look to a man or a woman for authority. The real authority for any teaching is its demonstrability and practicability. The very moment you begin to take the attitude toward life that there is a beneficent power, an all-knowing, omnipresent, omnipotent Being and let go of your personal effort, you find that this principle works. Through your own demonstration of the principle, you yourself become the authority for its authenticity.

In approaching the healing work, you must make the acknowledgment to yourself that even though the end and object of healing is to bring people to spiritual living, the proof that this is the way to spiritual living is in the healing that it brings into people's lives. The end and object we know and accept, but it is important that no one shirk the healing work. Do not try to evade the responsibility of healing work, stating disdainfully, "Oh, we're not concerned or interested in healing anybody!" We are! We are very much interested because today even as in the days of Jesus, the bringing out of harmony in mind, body, and pocketbook is the proof of the truth of the message.

When John the Baptist was in prison, he evidently became a little frightened and doubted that Jesus was all he thought he was, so he sent word and asked, "Art thou he that should come?"[6] In other words, "Are you this Christ? Are you this one we have been expecting?" Jesus did not reply, "Yes, I am"; nor did he show John a certificate from any rabbinical school. But he did say, "Go and shew John again those things which ye do hear and see: The blind receive their sight, and the lame walk, the lepers are cleansed, and the deaf hear, the dead are raised up, and the poor have the gospel preached to them."[7]

If there is any other proof of the rightness of spiritual truth, if there is any other measuring rod, you have to go outside the teaching of Christianity for it. In Christianity there is only one measuring rod: "Go and shew John." Through this truth the sick are healed. Jesus never felt so superior that he was unwilling to heal the multitudes and supply them. He did not set himself up on a pedestal. He stayed right there with his people where they were and met their needs on their level. He even stopped the storm at sea.

A man named Jesus did this through the power of the Christ in him. Many of you have seen this same power operate in these modern days: You have seen the Christ actually stop storms at sea and in the air and lift fogs on the highway. This, you have seen too many times to doubt that the Christ meets your problems right where you are. It does this not by your taking thought, but because It is the divine Comforter, the infinite Presence within your own consciousness.

The example of Jesus should be sufficient for you so that every time you are called upon for healing you will do all that you can to bring it about. This has nothing to do with whether or not a person is deserving of the healing. It has nothing to do with whether or not you like the person or whether he is living a life of which you approve or disapprove. If he comes to you for healing, you do the utmost you can. You use the highest under-standing you have to bring it about.

That does not mean letting some people use up your time and energy in sitting around, arguing about the truth or the pros and cons of spiritual healing. These people deserve to be healed, too, and in time they may overcome their tendency to argue, but for such people let your work be absent treatment.

Those to whom you give your time and whom you permit to take up your time should be those you feel are on this path because they want to know the truth of being and are hungry for it. If you have the bread and the water and the wine to give them, it will not make any difference whether you sit up all night or get up to go calling in the middle of the night or what you do. That is what you are here for; that is the reason you are in this work. But do not let your time be consumed by people who merely want to sit around and argue some philosophy of life, or prove how wrong you are, or how impossible spiritual healing is, or how much better some other system is. If they want help for healing or for supply, let them telephone you and ask for help and then give them the help absently, but you give your time and attention to those who humbly say, "Give me something to drink; give me this pearl of great price."

Every Case Can Be Met

You must take full responsibility in this work when calls come to you for help. You do not assume that the patient is not doing something that he should be doing, or that he is not grateful or sincere. You do your best. Be sure that you are grateful and sincere and do not worry about the patient's gratitude and sincerity. If he is ungrateful or insincere, he will pay his own penalty in whatever way it is. It is quite possible that he may get the healing, in spite of all his wrong doing or wrong thinking, so do not be critical of him. You assume the responsibility, and if you do not succeed, if you do not heal all your cases, then be honest enough to acknowledge, "Well, I guess I didn't rise high enough. If I had risen higher in consciousness, it would have been met."

After thirty years in the practice of spiritual healing, I can tell you that this is true: There is not a single case in the world that cannot be met. If one practitioner cannot meet it, some other practitioner can. You and I, however, are not always able to meet every case that comes to us because some of them demand a little higher state of consciousness than we happen to have at that moment. That does not mean that the case is incurable or that it cannot be met. It means that the particular practitioner has not risen high enough in a particular case to meet it. It does not mean that you and I will not bring through the healing of another or more difficult case tomorrow, but it does mean we may not have risen high enough to meet that particular one.

Therefore, if you do not meet a case, be willing to let the patient go on and find someone else, someone who can meet the problem for him. But do not ever believe that there is such a thing as a case that cannot be met and do not admit into your consciousness any fear about those cases that come to you.

One of the greatest difficulties in this work is the clearing out of previous beliefs about metaphysical practice and metaphysical truths. One of the greatest problems is to recognize that many former practices and beliefs were founded on superstition, on personal loyalty, or on personal conviction, rather than on the divine truth of being.

Impersonalization of Good and Evil

There have been people all through the ages who have known there was a God and who have been close to God, yet they have never achieved a personal demonstration of health and harmony. What I am about to tell you now is vitally important, even more important than simply feeling a sense of closeness to God and knowing that you are spiritual.

Too many people in the metaphysical world are still trying to reform men and women as well as heal and remove diseases. That is where the difficulty lies. They have not learned that there cannot be God *and* sin and disease. Anyone who believes that is still steeped in the old theological teaching of God and devil. The Infinite Way teaches that there is not God *and* devil; there is not God *and* sin, disease, and death; there is not God *and* man. There is only God appearing *as* individual being. The Infinite Way reveals that God is the life of you and the mind of you, and all that appears as sin or disease is but a universal belief which keeps hammering against your thought and which you first accept and then try to get rid of, but this belief is not *personal* to you or to anyone else.

The first half of our work is right identification, that is, realizing our spiritual identity and the infinity of our own being. The second half has to do with the impersonalization of error—not pinning evil onto a person and then trying to get rid of it. Remember the problem is that somebody is hypnotized and, in his state of hypnotism, is asking you to remove his "white poodle." Do not be in a hurry to rush out to do this because that will be a clear indication that you, too, are hypnotized, and that then would be a case of the blind leading the blind.

The only way you can help is by keeping yourself dehypnotized and realizing, "Thank You, Father; I know there is no poodle to be removed." It is like the story found in ancient scripture: If you were in a little boat on the river, and another little boat came along with no one in it and bumped into you, you would not become angry. You would realize that an accident had occurred and you would do something about adjusting it. That would be the end of it. But, suppose you thought that there was a man in the boat. Then you might become angry and blame the man because he had bumped into you, nearly hurting you and wasting your time, but then when you looked a second time you discovered that there was only an empty boat. How could you vent your anger on an empty boat?

That is the point: A person comes to you and tells you that he is sick, and immediately you try to do something about the person, but the error is not a person at all. It is just a belief, an impersonal error, not personal to the individual.

So, in your everyday experience, if a little boat starts coming toward you, do not become angry or get upset. Instead, make an adjustment through your realization that it is nothing. When a person tells you that he is sick or sinning or fearful, try to visualize that empty boat in which there is no person. In the same way, there is no person who is sick, sinning, or fearful; therefore, there is no purpose served in arguing with a person, trying to correct or heal him or reprimand him.

Do not become hypnotized with the appearance of a "white poodle." There isn't any! Do not become hypnotized with an appearance called a disease or a sin. There isn't any! It is always an appearance. You must learn to be quick in your realization that it is only an appearance and that you cannot do anything to that non-existent "white poodle," just as you could not do anything to an empty boat.

The more quickly you learn to treat every problem that comes to you in that way, the better healing work you will do. One of the reasons more healing is not being done in the metaphysical field is that too much attention is being paid to the healing, the changing, correcting, or improving of people, to the getting rid of sin or of disease. The whole metaphysical world has become mesmerized with the appearance, instead of developing or teaching practitioners not to be fooled by the appearance.

Be done with the sending out of thoughts to people because all you are doing is manipulating the human mind. Do not do it. If you have to treat, treat yourself. Treat yourself against the belief that God ever created a mortal anywhere on earth to be sick or sinful. And if God did not create a mortal, there are no mortals. Then that whole picture that is presenting itself to you is like that "white poodle"—illusion.

Unless you make use of both parts of this particular unfoldment—right identification and the impersonalization of good and evil—you are not following this teaching. Do not try to parallel it with any other. Try to take this as it is of itself and either make it work or if you find you cannot, then admit, "Well, I guess I was on the wrong track"; or, "It wasn't for me." But do not try to "work it in." Do not try to see how it fits in with whatever other metaphysical teaching you may have been studying. It will not work. There are too many things in the other teachings which would only befog the issue.

In proportion as you learn and practice the basic principles of the Infinite Way, will you find this teaching practical in your experience. First of all, remember the infinite nature of your own being as the very *I Am* of

God; and secondly, the absolute nothingness of sin, disease, and death, realized through your ability to impersonalize these errors, and to see that they do not exist as persons, conditions, or places, but only as illusion or suggestion.

*The secret of harmony, whether of health or wealth, is the impersonalization of good and the impersonalization of evil.**

---

*For a complete exposition of the subject of spiritual healing, see the author's *The Art of Spiritual Healing*, ©1975 by Emma A. Goldsmith (Lakewood, CO: Acropolis Books, Inc., 1997).

~ 8 ~

QUESTIONS AND ANSWERS

Question: Is there any way of judging as to when a practitioner should take a case or have the person go to someone else?

Answer: From the very moment that a practitioner takes hold of a case, something begins to happen. Within twenty-four hours he knows, and the patient knows, whether there is a feeling of something at work. If there is not and the patient has any urge at all to change practitioners, let him go; or if the practitioner himself can see that within a day or two or three there is any sign that the patient would like to make a change, he should encourage it. The wisest thing in the world is for a practitioner never to believe that a patient belongs to him, or, in other words, that he has "a patient."

No patient is mine beyond the call that he has just this minute made. Five minutes later he is free to go to anybody else with no feeling on my part. I do not believe that there should be such a thing as personal feelings in the relationship between practitioner and patient. A person, who may be a patient this minute and ask for help, is under no compulsion to come back and explain tomorrow that he wants another practitioner. He is not obligated to me one moment beyond the minute he has asked for a treatment. If he comes back the next day, he comes of his own accord; but I have absolutely no hold on him and want none.

Sometimes I have had cases that do not seem to respond immediately, but the patient says, "I want you to go on with the work." In a case like that, you can be sure he is feeling something or he would not want the work to be continued. The healing may not have come through, but nevertheless there is something which causes the patient to say, "No, I want you." There is some bond. As long as he wants your help, continue the work; but at the first indication that you are not making any progress, and he realizes it, let him know that he is released and free and that he is not to feel any attachment or obligation to go on with you. In this work, it is all according to the inner response you feel.

Question: How far do you go with patients if they want *materia medica* help or want to resort to medicine?

Answer: That is a question that has to be answered by the individual case at the time. For example, my background being what it is, I naturally do not believe that we should mix medicine and metaphysics. On the other hand, it is apparent that many cases and situations are not being met through spiritual help. Many metaphysicians wear glasses, which certainly is a reliance on *materia medica.* This is a "suffer it to be so now" with them because it is undoubtedly better to wear glasses than it is to go around half blind waiting until the demonstration is made. However, even though glasses continue to be used, no one should be satisfied to accept this condition permanently; he should always continue his efforts to free himself.

Similarly, there are people who, in their early stages of coming into metaphysics from *materia medica,* may be taking sleeping powders or depending on digitalis or insulin, which according to *materia medica* "is keeping them alive." If they are young in the work, my procedure is not to upset them about that, but to do my work and free them from these material dependencies. But if I do not free them very quickly and I see that they are going to keep clinging and clinging and clinging to these dependencies, then I let them go.

If someone comes who has a cancer or a condition which, unless surgery is performed, would result in death, according to medical belief, or when there may be a broken bone and the patient wants to have it set, in my opinion it is far better for the patient to resort to surgery, get it over with, and get back on the path than to die because of a superstitious belief that it is better to die than to undergo surgery.

Every time, however, that you go back to *materia medica* you are failing in your demonstration. As I have said before, when I do not meet a case, I am honest enough to acknowledge that in that particular case I did not rise high enough. I offer no alibis. Whatever the case, I am sure that Jesus would have met it, and that indicates that anyone with the fullness of the Christ-mind could have met it.

There is no use dodging the issue. So I freely admit, "Well, I didn't rise high enough, but I'm going to keep on in this work and try to do better next time."

So, if someone comes along with a fear so great that he feels he must undergo surgery, or as often happens, he or she may not particularly want it but may have a wife, husband, mother, son, or daughter who insists on medical attention and who may feel honestly: "No, we're not going to let you take this risk; you have to have medicine"; then stand by with those people–they need your help more than ever.

If someone that you know in this work has failed to make his demonstration and has had to go to a hospital, stand by with him. Your spiritual help may pull him through where the hospital or the surgery would not. Never cast off any person. Always remember this, and again Jesus is my authority, "Therefore all things whatsoever ye would that men should do to you, do ye even so to them."[1] If you yourself should reach the point where you could not make the grade and felt you needed some medical aid and found it necessary to go to a hospital, would you want your practitioner to refuse to help you? Would you want him to say, "You are in a hospital, so I wash my hands of you?"

Furthermore, suppose someone you know falls from grace, commits some crime, and is arrested. What are you going to do? Are you going to say, "Ho, ho! I'll have nothing to do with you!" No! That's the time he needs you more than ever—when he is in the deepest trouble. Jesus said, "I was sick, and ye visited me: I was in prison, and ye came unto me."[2]

My attitude is entirely different when people become chronically dependent on *materia medica*. If they are habitually taking sleeping powders, cathartics, and all the other remedies prescribed for an ailing body, they are not on this path, because obviously they are seeking only the "loaves and fishes." Remember how the people came to Jesus the next day after he had just fed them with the bread and the fishes, seeking to be fed again. It was then that he said in substance, "What are you looking for? Not the truth. You saw the miracle of the loaves and the fishes and you want some more of that."

No Infinite Way worker should cater to people who want to try a little of both *materia medica* and spiritual help. How can such people be helped? But with those who are beginners, stand by and have patience with them until they demonstrate their freedom. Remember, it is not a crime or an irredeemable failure to be unable to make a demonstration. What we have to do is to begin again. Many of us are required to repeat a grade in school, and that is what sometimes happens in this work. We go along and think we are making remarkable progress, and then all of a sudden something comes along and there are our feet of clay. But that is when we need our friends on the spiritual path the most.

So that is my attitude. Do not cater to the medical thought and do not go along indefinitely with people who are trying to benefit continuously by both *materia medica* and spiritual help. But on the other hand, do not reject anyone because he is failing in a demonstration. Rather stand by and help him get back on this path, because love is the principle of this work.

Question: If God is mind, or even if He is consciousness, is His activity not mental?

Answer: No, mental activity is a reasoning and a thinking activity. Consciousness is not a mental activity; consciousness does not reason or think: It is just aware.

Two times two is four. God, infinite Consciousness, does not use a mental process in arriving at that answer. It is just a state of *is*. There has never been a time when it was other than that, nor was there ever a time in creation when two times two *became* four. There is no process of making two times two, four, and, therefore, no mental activity is necessary to establish that fact. Two times two has always existed as four, and the only mental activity involved in that concept is the activity of awareness.

When I stated that we do not work on the mental plane, what I meant was that the only activity of the mind is one of awareness. We become aware that we are spiritual, that we are divine being, that sin, disease, and death are illusions—just nothingness, or mesmeric suggestion—but we do not go through any mental process to make this so.

We do not indulge in any kind of a mental process with the idea of making a sick man well or a poor man rich or an unemployed man employed. If there is any process at all, it is the process of awareness, the process of becoming aware of that which already divinely is, and that is not a mental process.

From the human standpoint, we cannot look at a sick person and mentally assert, "You are well." That is hypocrisy and ignorance and is obviously untrue. It is only with inner spiritual discernment that we can look through the human appearance and see the divine reality which underlies that appearance. So it is not through a mental process that we become aware of perfection, and our work is to become aware of perfection. It cannot be done humanly with the human mind because nothing that the human mind will ever know will be perfect. It is only when the human mind is not at work, when in the very stillness of our innermost being, our Soul-senses and spiritual awareness are aroused, that we behold the perfect man.

That is why spiritual healing is not a mental process. None of your or my thinking will add health to you or to me. Again we go back to Jesus: "Which of you by taking thought can add one cubit unto his stature?"[3] Who by taking thought can make "one hair white or black?"[4] "Take no thought for your life. . . ."[5] In other words, a mental process has nothing to do with spiritual truth, and that is really the crux of this whole presentation of truth. Human mental activity has nothing whatsoever to do with this particular approach. No amount of knowing the truth will help you—no amount of declaring the truth. No human mental process enters into this presentation.

The Infinite Way is concerned first and foremost with the development of the Soul-sense. When we are still, sitting back with that "listening ear," when we are in meditation, giving what we call a treatment, the inner Thing comes to life and shows us the inward spiritual perfection, and that outwardly becomes interpreted as a healthy, sane, or wealthy human being.

Right there is the meat and the substance of the whole Infinite Way. We do not indulge in any mental processes for self-improvement, and that is where we depart from the entire metaphysical field. It is a question of developing our spiritual sense so that ultimately we arrive at the consciousness of a Jesus Christ who could look at the cripple and say, "Rise up and walk!"[6]

What do you think would enable a man to say that? Do you think any mental process anyone could use would instantaneously raise up a crippled man so he could walk? No, only the divine Fire within, only the very Spirit of God could do that.

It might be possible to give a person a year's treatment and gradually turn him from a cripple into a healthy man by mental manipulation—by a pounding and pounding and pounding away at him mentally. But no human being could instantaneously do that—only the fire of God in him.

That is why we must make love the dominating influence in our experience. All the divine qualities of

the Christ must become active in us; all personal de-
sires—all hate, envy, criticism, and condemnation—must be
relinquished. There can be no indulgence in those human
qualities. We must not fear them, for we are then missing
the opportunity to bring forth the divine qualities of the
Christ. Why should we go around indulging in these
human things at the expense of cheating ourselves of
having that mind that was in Christ Jesus?

The mind that was in Christ Jesus does not engage in
any reasoning or thinking process. To the palsied man it
says, "Arise, and take up thy bed, and walk,"[7] and might
have added, "What is to hinder you? Is there any power
apart from God?" This mind of Christ Jesus is awareness
without a process.

The truth is that there is no power apart from God,
but we could say it and say it and say it, and nothing
would happen. In fact, a metaphysical teacher may sit
and talk these truths from now until doomsday and not
bring out any measure of spirituality in his class; or a
clergyman may preach spellbinding sermons and yet the
members of his congregation go on being the same kind
of human beings year in and year out, with just as many
ills, just as many crimes, just as much cheating in business, just as much corruption in politics. Why are not the
congregations in these churches and centers improved
spiritually? For the simple reason that they are sometimes hearing only an intellectual presentation of truth,
and even though many times this comes from a very
good human being, if that person has not a developed
Christ-consciousness, or spiritual sense, he cannot
quicken the minds and hearts of his followers.

What is most important is not to criticize the human
faults, but rather to lift people up to the place where they

are not human any more. You cannot do that by means of human reason. You can tell a person not to steal; you can tell a person not to lie or cheat; you can tell him anything you want to tell him, and many of you probably have, but usually it has not and does not have any effect upon his conduct.

Improved conduct is only brought about by reaching the individual through the Spirit. You must attain such a degree of spirituality that when a sinner is touched by your consciousness, he loses all desire to sin. When that happens, you are functioning as a spiritual teacher. You are then not teaching new truths and new mental processes: You are giving forth the age-old truth that has been tried and found effective—effective by Elisha, Elijah, and Isaiah, by Jesus and John.

Truth is so simple that it can all be summed up in less than one thousand words, but it is only through developing our own spiritual qualities that spirituality can be brought out in those we meet.

Question: Why does God take us down into "Egypt?"

Answer: God is not a person sitting around manipulating the world: God is our very own consciousness. God is forever imparting Its truth and Its guidance to us, but because we are not always listening, sometimes we are compelled to take a roundabout way to reach our goal. It is not God who is responsible for this: It is our own obtuseness. God is always right where we are, imparting His impulses until ultimately we reach the goal.

It is not that there was a God who made his brothers sell Joseph into slavery, but undoubtedly there was such a state of consciousness in Joseph that ultimately he was destined to be the king's right-hand man, and in some way, he had to be brought to the proper place in order to function in that capacity. Similarly, the circumstances which we define as our "Egypt" may later be responsible for our becoming a "prince." In other words, had we not had some particularly trying experience, we would not have learned the necessary lesson, heard the Voice, and set our feet again upon the path.

You can take all you have read so far in this book and immediately begin to put it into practice and gradually, through that understanding, come into perfect harmony; or, on the other hand, you can say, "Yes, I'll practice as much of it as I can, but I must indulge in this bit of humanhood today, or I must indulge in that." True, you arrive at your proper place ultimately, but often only through much suffering.

For example, you could at this moment stand on this truth: "All that the Father has is mine, and never again do I have to take thought for supply." You could take that stand right now and demonstrate it, but most of you will not do this. Most of you will be a little bit worried about next month's bills and continue to take thought for this, that, or the other thing; and to the degree that you take thought, you are violating your understanding. To that degree, then, there will be a period of suffering, though ultimately you will arrive at your goal.

That is what happened to Joseph. Had he been sufficiently attuned, he might have said: "I think I'll move to Egypt." But he didn't. Instead, he perhaps thought that he was always going to remain with his father and his brethren, so he had to be picked up and forced into his rightful place—Egypt.

Then when he was in the household of the Pharaoh, he could just as well have said to himself, "I am going to live as pure spiritual being and never let mortality enter my thought." But he didn't. He had to go down into prison and there learn that the indulgence of any form of mortality has no place in the experience of a spiritual being. When he was in prison, he had time to think, and that is when he finally came to the realization, "Well, if I'm spiritual, I guess I'd better act like it." Sometimes it takes the very depths of human experience to bring us to an awareness where we are willing to let the spiritual light gleam.

Question: I was called to the bedside of a very sick man, and I began with the first chapter of Genesis, explaining to him the perfection of God's creation. I then asked him if he could accept what I had told him, and he replied in the affirmative. The man who had taken me there asked me to work for him for a couple of days, which I did. How do you account for the healing in such a situation?

Answer. I would say that it had to do with your receptivity to truth, which is the highest form of treatment there is, but when we begin to work mentally and then call it God-healing, it is ludicrous. When we reach a state of receptivity, however, so that when any case comes, the ear is open, and the impartation comes like a flash, telling us how to work or what truth to reveal, then that is God-healing.

Question: Then you think that was God healing?

Answer: There is no question about it, because it came to you without any thought process; it was not conscious thinking. It was a state of receptivity which revealed that truth to you. This, I call being divinely led, because it did not consist of sitting down and giving a treatment to a disease or a condition. I do not believe in that kind of treatment. Turn to God and let God show you the need of the moment.

Can you imagine what a man wrongly imprisoned would feel if I told him that there is no injustice, that man is perfect? He would want to throw such words right back at me. But when one is led to tell him the story of Joseph and his brethren, then he might begin to understand the spiritual sense of forgiveness. The higher sense of forgiveness is looking through the human being and his activity and seeing that there at the center of his being sits God, which at the moment is being misinterpreted.

In all treatment, never do I permit myself to think a thought, to make a denial, or to affirm a truth. I take the attitude: "Speak, Lord; for thy servant heareth. . . ."[8] Be still, and know that I am God."[9]

Take the attitude that this is God's universe; let God do something about it; be a witness to God in action. Then you are led to say the right thing, think the right thing, or do the right thing.

That is how the book, *The Letters,* came into existence. Whenever letters came from patients out of town asking for help, no matter what the problem was, I would sit down and turn within and let the Father speak. Then I would write a letter to the patient about the problem, but I always exemplified a particular point of what we call truth. The more you live in this state of receptivity, the more you live and develop this receptive ear, the more the divine Voice will speak to you at every point and at every call, although not always in words.

Jesus' words are literally true: "I can of mine own self do nothing . . . If I bear witness of myself, my witness is not true.[10] . . . My doctrine is not mine, but his that sent me."[11] That is our attitude. As human beings, we do not have enough power even to heal a simple cold. The power is that divine Impulse, that Thing we call God, or the Christ.

The only way we can bring the Christ to bear on a case is to set aside our human thinking and permit ourselves to become the vehicle for the activity of the Christ. Then the right words come, the right thoughts, or the right feeling.

Throughout these many years, I have observed with so many different kinds of cases that if I could just be receptive enough, the answer would come with the first call for help, and the results would be instantaneous. But in other cases it might require a second or a third call. Sometimes, it may even take two or three years. It all depends on the situation. I have had cases that have been long-drawn out and which took a great deal of patience and long hours of work. There have been cases where, in the beginning, I have had as many as ten, fifteen, or twenty telephone calls in a twenty-four-hour period—incessant calls. Then I would watch as these calls gradually decreased from ten to five to two and then one every other day, and so on.

The process was always the same, always letting the Christ do the work, letting this inner infinite Thing we call the Christ—the Comforter, the Holy Ghost, the Spirit of truth—do the work and not trying to make of myself a mental worker using mental processes or treatments. While the mental approach may probably work for some people on certain levels of consciousness, it is not the approach of the Infinite Way.

None of this is said in any spirit of criticism, condemnation, or judgment, but only from the viewpoint that mental activity has nothing to do with the particular approach to truth as taught in the Infinite Way. And naturally, I do believe that this approach will bring the greatest reward. The reason this work has grown and spread so rapidly is because the results do come, and they come because of this infinite Thing which dispels the illusion.

Question: Can we all develop this receptivity?

Answer: Yes, we can all develop it, according to the degree of our faithfulness to the principles. It is, however, a major work to which we must devote our lives, giving up everything of a distracting nature, everything of a material nature, and everything of an interfering nature. You have to put your whole life into this thing. This is not something that can be accomplished by the simple desire to do it. The intent of this book is not to let you sit back comfortably and enjoy an hour or so of interesting reading, but to shake you from head to foot out of your human peace into an activity which makes that shake-up welcome. If it does that, from then on it is really work.

It means the giving up of time and money. It is something into which you put everything, if it is to be worth anything. It is arriving at that place where Christ lives in you, and if that is desirable to you, you have to work for it.

Going from a human being to a spiritual being is not accomplished in one bound. Even Saul of Tarsus had to seek the truth for years and years and years under a Hebrew teacher. He was seeking God, his heart was right, and because his purpose was to find the truth, no matter how erroneously he made his way, ultimately his life was transformed in one blinding flash, and he saw the Christ.

So with us. It does not matter what path we have been following. What really counts is the degree of earnestness with which we are seeking truth. Can we agree that we are no longer seeking a demonstration of things, but are seeking the consciousness of the presence of God and the willingness to let the things be added?

In that earnestness we will develop spiritual consciousness. That is why I have emphasized that in addition to your periods of meditation, there are three essentials on this path: One is a teacher who has caught some measure of the Christ and who can keep listening and listening and guiding and guiding; the second is reading inspirational, metaphysical, or scriptural writings which appeal to you and meet your need, not the reading that is good for somebody else, but reading that is good for you; and third, grasping every opportunity to gather together in groups with people who, without any selfish motive, meet for the purpose of learning more about God.

Every time you go to a metaphysical meeting or a church meeting, you are in the company of people whose main purpose in life is seeking God, no matter which path they may follow. It is possible to meditate and feel a sense of that Christ-peace in any church and to be happy with groups of people of any faith. The important thing is to be among people who love God and truth and are seeking it in some way. If your desire is for God, you will find God!

~9~

The Argument or Treatment

If the teacher of spiritual wisdom could sit and hear in the silence and then let the divine Consciousness impart the truth to his students, there would be little possibility of any misunderstanding, but because words cloak the real meaning, it is necessary for the student to discern the meaning between the lines.

As you know, I myself do not use affirmations and denials, and I disapprove heartily of their use in this work. Such things as reciting any statement, however scientific it may appear to be, twenty-five or a hundred times, or repeating the Lord's Prayer ten times, or affirming, "Every day prosperity is making me rich," are decidedly no part of the Infinite Way. That statement needs clarification, however, because the argument is used in this work and is that part of the work which I call treatment. Most of the time, you may use very little treatment, but on the other hand, there are occasions when you may use a great deal of treatment.

Ordinarily in the course of the day when a call for help comes over the telephone or by letter, very little in the way of treatment should be necessary because the state of consciousness in which the practitioner or teacher lives and which he maintains should be sufficient to meet all needs. It must be realized that the call for help has nothing to do with a person; it is just suggestion. Most healings are brought about through nothing more nor less than some such statement as, "I will be with you," or, "I will take care of it," or, "I am standing by," but back of those statements is the consciousness of truth, spoken or unspoken.

It must be understood, of course, that *I* means God. When a practitioner assures the patient, "I am standing by," he means that God is standing by and, therefore, his patient is in the best hands in the world. However, it would be very dangerous if the practitioner made such a statement merely as a human being, because, as a human being, the practitioner can do nothing for his patient, and every dedicated practitioner is well aware of this.

Even Jesus the Christ said, "I can of mine own self do nothing[1] . . . the Father that dwelleth in me, he doeth the works."[2] This divinely realized state of consciousness, a consciousness that is developed through hours and hours and hours of study, of meditation and prayer, and of living above sense testimony, does the work.

Meet the Calls at the Point of Contact

Most of the healing work for which I have been the instrument has been accomplished at the very moment of the call for help. Every request for help must be met at the instant of the call, so never tell anyone that you will give him a treatment tonight or an hour from now. Tonight may never arrive. Meet your cases and meet them now.

It is just as possible for you to give a treatment in a crowded room as it is when you are alone at home. You can give a treatment riding in a streetcar or when you are sitting at your desk, talking to one patient while giving a treatment to another. The reason for this is that you have no thought to direct to anybody, and you do not have to "hold" any right thoughts or send out any right thoughts.

All that is necessary is to be still and realize within your being: "Am I fooled by appearances? Do I believe there is a power apart from God? Is there more than one life? Is not that one life, God? Is this not just universal belief coming to me, trying to make me believe that it is a person or a condition, when all the time it is hypnotism, hypnotic suggestion? It is that 'white poodle' that does not exist, just as neither the disease nor the person exists, because all that exists is the divine Life that appears *as* person."

Calls for help must be met as they come to you. If, twenty or thirty minutes later, an hour or two, or six hours later, the patient comes back to your thought, either without any message from him or because he has made a contact by telephone or telegram, again you have to meet this situation in some way. As long as that person or his problem keeps coming to your attention, you have to meet it. You can meet it in the absolute without words or thought, if you are in a high enough state of consciousness; or, if you are not satisfied that the healing has taken place, you may have to close the door of your office, sit there alone, and go into meditation. You may have to reach the center of your being and call out, "Father, Father, reveal Thyself! Let me feel the reality of Being."

So you continue in that meditation or in that silence with your mind stayed on God—not on the patient or his claim—pondering God until the answer comes, until something within you responds, "It is done!" This response may not necessarily come in words, but you have the feeling of completeness, of a sense of healing, or of such complete freedom from the person and the problem that even if he called ten minutes later to recount again his worries, you would pay no attention to it because you have already had your answer. It may take him ten minutes or ten hours before he is aware that he has been healed, but as far as you are concerned, you are free from any further concern about that case, because the healing took place the moment this thing released itself within you.

I have had the experience of having to sit up all night, meditating and pondering some statement of truth, lying down and taking a nap for fifteen or twenty minutes, getting up again, then pondering, reading, or meditating for two hours, and perhaps beginning all over again, until the answer came.

Some practitioners and teachers have their work so organized that every week they can go away for two or three days and sit up on the mountain top with God, just as Jesus went away for forty days. But some of us have not yet been able to arrange our affairs so that that is possible. We may have to take our mountain top experiences sitting in our homes or offices or when the world is asleep at night. Failure to take time for these experiences is one of the reasons why occasionally claims come which catch us unprepared spiritually, and the answer does not come as quickly as it should.

When a call comes to you after you have had days and days of intensive, inspirational, and Soul-lifting study or association with others on the Path—days which have raised you to a high state of consciousness—you will find that you scarcely know whether the cases presented to you are hard or easy: They just melt away.

But often when we are in the routine of our particular work, we are not always in that high place, and for that reason, error makes itself apparent to us as if it were a horrible devil. Those are the times when it is difficult to realize the nothingness of evil, but that is when we have to stick with the truth.

Treatment Illustrated

Suppose some case of an apparently serious nature is presented to me. Immediately I might think about life and God: I would realize that there is only one life, and that life is God, and because it is the only life, life must be eternal, must be infinite, must be omnipresent, and that life must be the life of every individual. Therefore, nowhere in heaven or on earth could there be an impaired life, a diseased life, a dead life, a paralyzed life, or a sinful life. Only mesmeric suggestion can testify to error, and that is reversed in the understanding of one Consciousness.

So thought would go from one truth to another, and then finally it would stop, and there would be left only an awareness of life as God. That is an example of treatment or the use of argument.

I would not treat the person; I would not treat the condition: I would treat myself. I might even talk to myself, "Now, what is this thing that is touching me? This is just nothing but a suggestion coming to me of a selfhood apart from God. This is nothing more nor less than that hypnotist trying to make me believe that there is a 'white poodle' when I know in my heart and soul that there is no such thing. Why, of all people, should I believe that there is such a thing as mortality or fear? Why should I believe that there is a mind apart from God?"

I would then sit and wait until the contact is made. It is just as if there is a little "click," a breath, and when I catch something like that, I have a complete sense of release and can get up and feel sure that all is well with the patient. And it usually is.

Such use of the argument in many cases is necessary, and it is legitimate for you to use it any time any appearance of error comes to you. It is right for you to sit down and realize, "What is this coming to me? Is this not a couple of streetcar tracks that are trying to make me believe they come together? I do not have to accept that! Is there somebody telling me there is a 'white poodle' or a black one or a pink one? I do not have to accept that! This is nothing more nor less than the actual presence of God, appearing as material sense and its formations, and it is up to me to reinterpret it. There is nothing but the presence of God—God, infinite and all. There is nothing else!"

That might be the end of the treatment, but that does not conclude your work. Treatment, or the argument, lifts you up to where you can apprehend, or catch, the word of God as it comes to consciousness. All you have done in treatment is to reassure yourself mentally that the appearance is not real, but you have not yet prayed, you have not yet felt the Christ. What you are interested in achieving is the realization of the Father within, of the Christ that liveth in you, the actual awareness of the presence and power of God, which dispels the illusion of sense.

Hypnotism, the Substance of Human Appearances

All error is hypnotism claiming to operate as your own thinking. As soon as you realize that the error is not in your thinking or in that of your patient, you separate yourself from the suggestion and become free. Recognizing the error, regardless of its form, as universal hypnotism, or mesmeric suggestion, which claims to act as your own thought or thinking, is the release. As long as the error is not recognized as suggestion or imposed hypnotism, you will remain in sin, disease, lack, or limitation. Every appearance of sin or disease, lack or death is but hypnotism claiming to act as your thinking. The realization of this truth is your remedy.

Every claim or suggestion of mortality, even good mortality, must be dealt with in this way. These human appearances, which are the activity of mesmerism, must be understood as the finite or unillumined sense of mind and mind's formations. This reversal and reinterpretation of the picture completes the treatment and reveals divine harmony where error had seemed to be.

To be a practitioner or teacher, one must in some measure have been released from this universal hypnotism so that one stands back of this world, as it were, and "sees" with the unhypnotized mind. To this illumined consciousness, mesmerism is not power. It never was real power, but it operated as both presence and power until it was detected and cast out through the realization of the one Self as the all-power.

Remember that hypnotism always appears as person, place, thing, circumstance, or condition. Therefore, again I repeat, never give a treatment to a patient or a condition: Give yourself a treatment in order to reinterpret the appearance.

Maintaining Your Spiritual Integrity

Many of you, however, may not find it necessary to use treatment as such in your healing work. Some of you may be able to take that higher step of sitting in the silence with that ear of expectancy, letting the answer come. When a claim of any kind presents itself to you, sit down and find the center of your own being. You might take the word, God, or Christ, or Truth, and keep it in your thought, always bringing your thought back to it and continuing until that awareness comes.

This is a higher form of treatment than using the argument, and you can eliminate the argument, if you keep yourself in a high enough spiritual state. You cannot do it, however, if you are continuously coming down to the mortal level of living, watching movie thrillers, reading lurid novels, and indulging in all the material sense experiences with which the majority of people fill their time and mind. Do not think you can give part of your time to such materialistic living and at the same time be in a state of spiritual consciousness where you will not need to use the argument in treatment. It cannot be done. You have to live on a higher plane than that.

That does not mean that you have to leave the world. You can remain in your business or social world and still live on a spiritual level; but you cannot fill your mind with cheap movies, horror-ridden novels, sensational newspaper accounts, and degrading comics and still maintain a spiritual attitude. To maintain a spiritual attitude, you must remember, "Thou wilt keep him in perfect peace, *whose mind is stayed on thee.*"[3] You must learn to live as much as possible in the atmosphere of the Christ.

If you are on this path, you are *in* the world but not *of* it; and while it is quite natural and right to want to be a good citizen and decide whom you would like to see elected and then go out and vote for him, do not let it trouble you if he does not get elected. That is not your problem at all. If you are depending on spiritual consciousness for your security, you will be safe no matter who is at the head of the government. Your responsibility is to realize continuously the true nature of God, whether appearing as officials of the government, relatives, neighbors, friends, or enemies.

Your problem is you—and that is not selfishness. The reason you are important and the reason it is necessary for you to keep your spiritual integrity is because one person on this path can provide safety, security, and strength for thousands. Keeping your mind off the human problems of the world and stayed on spiritual values may affect tens of thousands of people, possibly not in the way you think it should affect them, but ultimately in the right direction. No matter how far you go on this path, your human judgment in outlining the direction you want to take may still be wrong. Not only should you not outline for yourself or for anyone else, but you should not permit anyone to do so for you.

The Mind of the Practitioner Is the Mind of the Patient

You have no right to let anybody manipulate your thoughts, handle your thoughts, or send thoughts to you. Never! Do not let anyone take possession of your mind; do not ever surrender your mind to anyone. Jesus told us years and years ago not to fear that which could kill the body, but only that which could destroy the Soul. And nobody can destroy it more easily or more quickly than by taking possession of your mind and manipulating it.

If you were to ask me for help, I would never permit myself to be tempted to send a thought out to you. I would never be guilty of such practice. But I would sit down and feel this within-ness whereby I actually contact the Christ. But I can only make a contact with the Christ by going first to God, and then my contact with you is established. After that I can sit in joy, peace, and harmony.

It is like trying to reach someone on the telephone. No one can be reached without first going to central. After making that contact, I would just stay at the Central Office with God, and God, being the all-knowing Wisdom, the omnipotent Intelligence, knows where the call comes from, and He knows enough to make the contact with the proper person. I do not do it; God does it. All I do is go to the Center of my being, which is God.

There is only one mind. Therefore, the mind which is the mind of me is the mind of you. So when I go to the Center of my own being, there are not two people to send thoughts out, one to the other. There is just one infinite Person, called God, communing with His infinite children. That infinite Intelligence knows just who tuned in and why and what for, and the answer goes forth.

When I go to the Christ, I never permit myself to think of a human being, not even those who have asked for help. The mere fact that someone has asked for help or has reached out to me for help means that he has tuned in on his connection with the Central Office. My going to God is like going to central and so probably what happens is that we meet there. Then whatever God reveals to me, God reveals to the patient. I have not had anything to do with it at all except to be the one to go to God, to the Center of my being. There, we, as individuals meet, and it is there that the work is done. But it is done by God, by divine Love.

It is legitimate to use the argument in healing, but its purpose is not to establish something out here; it is merely to establish the awareness within you of the reality without. As a rule when some people make affirmations, it is for the purpose of making a sick person well. When a person takes a statement and repeats it a hundred times, he does so because he is convinced there is a sin or sickness and that much repetition is in some way going to heal it. But that is not our work.

This is not to say, however, that good healings have not been brought about through such a method of working, but personally I do not have too much confidence in the permanence of those healings because usually they are not spiritual healings. I have known some of the early metaphysical workers who really worked hard mentally, and often healing took place; but it was usually brought about by one mind overpowering another temporarily. We do not indulge in that type of work.

Our work is a realization that all there is, is God appearing *as* individual you and me. The treatment is not designed to change or improve anyone or anything out here. It is aimed at bringing to our consciousness the assurance and awareness of the already existing perfection. The wise practitioner is able to see behind the false, finite appearance because he sees with the unfettered mind, which is the instrument of God.

The sense which presents pictures of discord and inharmony, disease and death, is the universal mesmerism which produces the entire dream of human existence. It must be understood that there is no more reality to harmonious human existence than to discordant world conditions. It must be realized that the entire human scene is mesmeric suggestion and we must rise above the desire for even good human conditions.[4]

~ 10 ~

THE MISSION OF THE MESSIAH

For centuries, the Hebrews had watched eagerly for the coming of the promised Messiah. They were, of course, practically slaves of Caesar and were not too happy even with their church administration which was holding them under too tight a bond, so they had been scanning the skies for years for this new Messiah. They thought that with his coming they would be free of many of the tithes required of them by the church and of the taxes they were paying to Caesar, because the financial drain on them had grown to be a serious problem.

So naturally their expectancy was that, when the Messiah came, he would certainly dethrone Caesar and give them the Holy Land in which to live as a free people. Political freedom probably was uppermost in their minds, because then Palestine would become a political entity, free of the domination of Rome, and they would be a free people economically, politically, and nationally.

There is every indication that that is what they were expecting of their Messiah, but when Jesus came he did not give them the material freedom which they sought. In answer to all the requests and demands as to when this long awaited freedom would be given them, he answered, "My kingdom is not of this world."[1]

To free the Hebrews politically, economically, or nationally was not his mission, and that is perhaps the reason they rejected him. If Jesus had offered to lead an army against Caesar, they would probably have accepted him as their Messiah and their king. But that was impossible because that was not the nature of his mission. His ministry was a spiritual one, and what he was offering them was spiritual freedom, freedom from every kind of materiality. If the Hebrews had been able to accept this, it would have freed them from Caesar and from all the other bonds, because when people are spiritually free, they are physically and mentally free; but their vision did not go that far. They could not accept a Messiah with that kind of a message, so they rejected him.

Human Need Drives People to the Christ

Our spiritual ministry of today is similar in the sense that the people who turn to it are for the most part seeking relief from some kind of human bondage. If we were to tell our patients and students, "Let's see if I can demonstrate a better home for you to live in and a better job and a better wife or a better husband, or better children or a bigger income, or perhaps, establish a colony somewhere to give you freedom from the atomic bomb or a huge army to be sure the Communists do not gain control of the world," it would not be difficult to attract the multitudes.

It is easy to attract the multitudes with extravagant promises of a material nature, no matter how unrealistic they may be. People like to hear such things because that is the only kind of improvement the majority of people seem able to understand.

In every age, however, there are a few who catch the higher vision, but only a few; and of those few, only one or two catch enough of the vision to go right on up to the heights. It is a strange thing—this work. People, driven mainly by some need, come to this Christ-teaching, and when they catch a little glimpse of it, it is like a breath of fresh air, and they feel that this is what they have longed for always, this is where they want to be. And they mean it, at least they think they do.

But this path has a way of fulfilling people's human needs, of quickly supplying the amount of income which they consider adequate, or perhaps slowly, of producing the degree of health which they think is satisfactory. And that is where they rest. They stop there, and sometimes even pull away from the truth, or they rest on that level, satisfied to get so far and remain there.

In the cases of hundreds and hundreds of people with whom I have worked—hundreds and hundreds who have come a little way along the path—I have seen this one stop when he reached an income of fifty dollars a week, that one when he reached one hundred fifty, another when he reached two hundred fifty, or still another when he reached the place where his body did not pain him any more. One stopped when he or she found a wife or husband or moved into a more desirable social circle. I have seen over and over and over again how few there are who really persevere and stand by waiting for that "last hour"—for the highest degree of unfoldment attainable.

So the Christ-ministry, which is offered the world every day of the week is rejected. Every time anyone opens his Bible and reads: "But seek ye first the kingdom of God, and his righteousness; and all these things shall be added unto you,"[2] he is being offered that same spiritual ministry that was offered two thousand years ago and which the people of old rejected. Need I tell you how often people today reject this same Christ-ministry in favor of demonstrating things or persons? Why is this? Is it perhaps because these people are still bound to their material sense of living?

The Spiritual Life, a Joyous Life

If the world but knew it, there are pleasures in the spiritual realm that far transcend anything in the human—pleasures, joys, and harmonies; there are friendships that transcend any type of human relationship that has ever been known. It is worthwhile to stick to this path; it is worthwhile to set sail for uncharted seas, for the wide horizon, for the places that the average human being will never find, those things for which he will not give up material comforts, for which he will not surrender his human dependence on, and attachment for, family life.

"Man shall not live by bread alone."[3] The very moment anyone touches this inner realm, the spiritual consciousness, he does not live by food alone, nor by sleep alone. This does not mean that he does not enjoy food or pleasant surroundings. I have never seen anyone who caught the vision who became ascetic or unbalanced in any way.

To live the spiritual life does not mean to become sanctimonious, and it does not mean to live on a daily ration of a cup of milk or a few grains of rice. On the contrary, I have found, not only with myself, but with many others who have touched this higher consciousness, that they enjoy the choice things of life—interesting places, stimulating companionships, well-prepared food, and attractively furnished homes. The truth is that an awareness of this spiritual Presence and Power attracts the higher things and yet does not make one attached to them or enslaved by them. It is a great stride forward to know that we do not live by bread alone, that our inner life is fed more by our spiritual contact than by any of the human activities of life. So let us watch that we do not set our sights on a ministry which will promise us only more or better matter.

Living the Christian Life

This truth is not merely for the purpose of making sick people well or poor people rich, but to *awaken* even healthy and wealthy people to a reliance on spiritual power, spiritual security, and spiritual freedom, which is not dependent on the success of medical research or on any political ideology or economic system under which they may be living. This is the kind of freedom which Jesus sought to give the Hebrews, in contradistinction to the freedom from physical bondage which Moses had brought to his people. Everyone still remains under the Mosaic law, however, in the sense that he is clinging to economic and political security and to the extent that he has not yet found this spiritual security which would keep him safe regardless of where he is living or under what form of government.

To be a Christian means more than merely membership in a Christian organization or citizenship in a Christian country. It means *living the Christ-principle,* which means literally to pray for your enemies, to pray for those who persecute us or despitefully use us; it means to make a sincere effort to forgive our debtors even unto seventy times seven and to return love for hate. The Christ-life compels us to "put up the sword" and therefore to use no human force even in our own defense. *I believe in self-defense, e.g just war*

? The Christian life, however, is an individual one and is never forced upon another. We do not dictate our will to our neighbor; we "render . . . unto Caesar the things which are Caesar's"[4]; and if our nation calls upon us in time of war for military service or for the means of conducting war, we fulfill every demand made upon us and yet do it with no malice or hate or fear, and with no conviction that force is a real power.

All are Christians who accept the law and reality of spiritual power, whether they belong to a church or not. True Christians have no occasion to rely on human means and methods since they have the inner Presence to guide, direct, govern, heal, maintain, and protect. They have "meat to eat that ye know not of,"[5] that is, a substance, strength, and power not visible to the world– an inner reliance.

But the fact of the matter is that most Christians are more Hebraic than Christian. They believe in the Judaic teachings and usually have more knowledge of, and faith in, what is in the Old Testament than what is in the New. When a Christian is told that he dare not speak an ill word to his neighbor, no matter what his offense to him, he considers that as something transcendental, rather than as an actual teaching of Jesus Christ.

When some Christians are reminded about praying for their enemies, they do not seem to know that those passages are in the Bible or that those who accept the Christ-teaching are expected to act upon those laws. Christians are not always Christians. They read the story of the Good Samaritan and yet they often withhold help from somebody for personal reasons—perhaps because the person is a German, a Japanese, a Russian, a Catholic, a Jew, or a Negro. But whatever it is, they are not fulfilling the teaching of the ~~Master~~, Christ Jesus. His teachings unveil and reveal spiritual being, spiritual identity, and spiritual existence. *→ God Incarnate*

What do you expect and what do you want from your Messiah? Remember that *your Messiah ~~is the Christ of your~~ ~~own being~~*. *Son of God, Jesus Christ* The question for you to decide is whether or not you have arrived at that point where you can reject the temptation to demonstrate persons and things and turn to the Christ, to the Kingdom within, and attain your spiritual freedom. In turning to the spiritual life, you are seeking this inner Kingdom, this Christ within, this divine Presence, a spiritual freedom, which means freedom from material laws, from material activity, from material powers, whether the power is one of infection or contagion, or of stars, or anything that claims to have power.

There is a reason why you are on this path. Something has drawn you to this way of life, to this teaching; something has drawn you to the reading of this book. You have not been drawn because of your acquaintance or friendship with me, nor because of any great reputation I have as a writer. No, it is not for any of those reasons. It is because an indefinable something, an invisible communion, has brought reader and writer together on the inner and spiritual level. *Lord*

It is what the ~~Master~~, Christ Jesus, referred to when he said, "My sheep hear my voice."[6] It is what the Hindu mystic means when he looks at a person with this recognition, "You are my student;" and the student looks up and replies, "I have been looking for you for years!"

That is it! Did you ever stop to think that the Song of Solomon and other spiritual messages are written in the language of love because the whole relationship of teacher and student is a relationship of love? Such a sacred relationship cannot and does not come through the reasoning mind. When you find the teacher or teaching that is really yours, you recognize it at once, perhaps because of your inner communion. At any rate, it is a recognition—almost like meeting a person for the first time, looking him in the eyes and saying, "I think we are going to be friends forever." It is a communion on an inner level.

In other words, every day of the week, you will find those people, circumstances, and places attracted to you that you could not get along without, nor they without you. You will find yourself drawn to those places where you can be of the greatest service and at just the right moment. You are tuned in on an infinite spiritual telephone system, and it is Central that is sending out and making the contacts for you. You do not make them; Central sends out and makes them for you. When you are living this life, you always find that this Central Office, God, the ~~inner Consciousness of you~~ *Holy Spirit*, is really the dominating influence in your life. There is no thought of wanting or deserving anything. In fact, you do not take thought for anything; you just follow the leadings that are given you and you contact those individuals who are necessary to your fulfillment.

That is really the first step in spiritual living. You have taken the first step in being brought to the reading of this book. From here on, you will find people being drawn to you, and you being drawn to others. You will find yourself being brought to places, and places drawing you to them. You will say, "That is just the thing I would have loved to have—if I had thought about it." But it is always something greater than you could have thought about for yourself.

Our object is not just to gain a little knowledge with which we can stop a few pains or change the dates on a few tombstones. What we want is to learn how to live the life that Jesus came to show us. He did not come just to heal sick people or to raise the dead. That was only the proof that his message was true. The import of his message was that in the spiritual kingdom we are "joint-heirs with Christ" in God, we are of the household of God, fellow-citizens with the saints.

In other words, it is an entirely different life that we live on the inner plane—a joyous life. True, we are part of the outer world, but we have an inner activity. No matter where we may be, in any crowd, big or small, if any of us should meet, there would be a little smile pass between us. We have a few little secrets; we have learned a few little things about the world and about ourselves; and so no matter where we would meet—two of us or twenty-two of us—there would be just that little smile, as much as to say, "We know something, don't we?"

Yes, we do know something! We know a little bit more about the Christ; we know a little bit more about inner living; we know a little bit more about that Kingdom which is not of this world; and we know a great deal more about how to overcome the world. We know that in overcoming the world, all that we are doing is overcoming the beliefs that this world presents, beliefs in infection and contagion, discord, poverty, and in things outside of, and apart from, our own being.

We are learning more than that. We are learning that the Christ ~~was not a man~~. The Christ ~~is~~ a sense of divine

Christ is both human and divine

~159~

Love that flows between us and, if the world would let It, It would flow from man to man and woman to woman and flood the earth. Then there would never be one man desiring another man's property or his wife; there would never be one country desiring another country, or its labor, or natural resources.

God, the Central Office

There would be a feeling flowing through the world as it is flowing through those of us who have no thought except to be in God's presence, those who can begin to sense that inner divine relationship, that thread running from one to the other of the dedicated spiritual seekers of the world, and in the center of it all, God, the Central Office, with lines running out making us one in Christ Jesus.

The Body of Christ

Do you begin to see what it means to be one in Christ Jesus? We are all one in Love; we are all one in infinite Intelligence; we are all one in interest; *we are all one.* All that I have is thine, and all that you have is mine. Why? Because we all have access to the same Infinity, we are all "joint-heirs with Christ" in God. That is a fellowship in Christ, a kinship in Christ. There is an invisible bond that exists between us because we have tasted and touched—at least in a measure—this inner communion. The minute we have caught the tiniest vision of Christ-consciousness, we have meat, water, and bread; we have supply; we have friendship, companionship, and health.

"I have meat to eat that ye know not of."[7] *I have a substance ye know not of. Nothing outside of me can deplete me because I am being continuously filled and refilled from this infinite Storehouse within.*

I have something "this world" knows nothing of. That which keeps replenishing me continually is replenishing everyone, making everyone independent of what the outside world thinks and does. I have meat; I have substance; and I am not dependent on person, place, circumstance, or condition. I am dependent on nothing but the infinite nature of my ~~own being.~~ spiritual relationship with God.

If we can catch one tiny glimpse of this vision, and if for any reason we should wake up tomorrow morning without a single dime to our name, still our breakfast, lunch, rent, and everything else necessary would be provided as long as we have received our baptism, as long as the Holy Ghost has descended upon us, giving us the spiritual vision to discern the invisible nature of supply.

You may say, "Those are beautiful words!" And I will agree with you that they are nothing more than words—until you yourself catch the fire of them, until you yourself catch the feeling, "This is it!" Once this happens to you, once this clicks within you and you feel, "Ah, I am home!" you really know that you have meat the world knows nothing about.

Then you can truly say as did Jesus, "I have overcome the world,"[8] meaning, "I have overcome the need for the world's sources and resources. I have overcome the need for anything from the outer realm because I am being fed from within. I have meat ye know not of. I have a source of supply that the world knows nothing about."

In this consciousness, you can draw water from the well without a bucket. If you did not have a rope long enough to stretch down to the well to bring up water, this Christ-consciousness could pour water out of your very fingers. "And I, if I be lifted up from the earth, will draw all men unto me."[9] I, if I be lifted up will impart and bestow upon all those who are in and of my consciousness, something of that infinite Storehouse without depleting my own being. Jesus, with the consciousness of the "meat that ye know not of," fed thousands and still had twelve baskets full left over. So with us. We can keep on imparting and imparting and imparting and imparting and never, never, never find ourselves impoverished or depleted.

"I have meat to eat that ye know not of "[10]—I have an inner Presence, an inner Power, that meets every situation of human experience, whether for myself or another, whether for myself or five thousand others. It is not anything that I personally possess in the sense that I can withhold It from anybody. It is not anything over which I have the power to say, "I can give It to you or withhold It," nor have I the power to sell It. It is mine only in the sense that I am the particular wire over which It is running at the moment. I am the particular vehicle as which It is expressing—not through which, but as which this infinite Thing is appearing.

Those who are fellow-citizens of the household of God have become part of an infinite telephone system, a spiritual telephone system. They will always be one with each other and will always feel free to call upon one another, knowing that they are one in Christ Jesus, that the interest of one is the interest of all, and that because they have meat that the world does not know, meat in infinite quantity and in infinite form and variety, they can share it with one another freely. There is no reason to withhold it. It is always of a holy nature in the sense that it is not personal.

Those who are of the household of God will never make personal demands upon one another or ask for personal sacrifices. The only demand there is, is a spiritual demand:

The Father is in me, and I am in the Father, and you are in me, and I am in you.

I have an inner strength that never wavers. I have life eternal—I am life eternal. I am the very presence of God and I am blessing the world through my realization that this is true, not only of me, but of every individual in the world; and whether or not he has awakened to this truth, this is the truth of his being.

Once you have attained your Christhood, you will have attained your spiritual freedom. You are then free from every claim of mortality—sin, disease, lack, and limitation.

Fr. Thomas Keating:

"God and our true Self are not separate. Though we are not God, God and our true Self are the same thing.

When you truly love yourself, you become aware that your true Self is Christ expressing Himself in you."

~ 11 ~

SEEK THE ANSWER WITHIN

As you work and study and above all, as you meditate, you will find that the answers to most of the ques-
tions that may arise in your mind will be revealed to you
in meditation. Entirely different from the knowledge
gained through books is that which comes through
unfoldment or revelation.

A person to whom some spiritual truth has been
revealed may be said to know that specific truth, at least
as much as concerns that particular unfoldment, but
when he attempts to tell anyone else about it, it lacks the
authority of first-hand revelation, unless it is imparted by
an illumined consciousness, in which case it carries
conviction.

It is possibly not too broad a statement to say that the
majority of the people of the world know practically
nothing about the meaning of such apparent intangibles
as God, Christ, Truth, Light, or Grace. The little that can
be found in dictionaries and reference books is for the
most part merely a faint tracing of a tremendously deep
subject.

Let us assume that we know little or nothing about the
Christ. We do know this much, however, that the Christ
is not a man; we know that the Christ is not a historical
figure. We know that the Christ was not born at a
particular time, in a particular country, or of a particular

religion. We know that "before Abraham was, I am."[1]
Before Abraham, the Christ is. Even unto the end of the
world, the Christ is.

The Christ is not a person, but rather a presence. But
if anyone tried to heal somebody by means of that
explanation he would very likely fail because such
knowledge of the Christ would be merely in the realm of
the intellect. Too much of truth is intellectually known;
too little has been realized, and that is the reason for so
many failures in healing.

Our metaphysical study has convinced many of us
intellectually that this is a spiritual universe and that all
physical structure—good or bad, healthful or sick—is but
an illusory sense of the ever-present harmonious reality.

Sometimes it comes as a surprise that our "knowing" or
"affirming" this truth does not immediately produce
healing, but it must be understood that no change is
produced in the visible universe merely through an
intellectually perceived truth. Until truth becomes a
realized state of consciousness through inner unfoldment,
no change in the outer circumstance will appear.

Spiritual healing is an activity of consciousness, not of
the intellect. It is the perception spiritually of that which
appears to sight materially. What appears outwardly as
a physical condition, good or bad, must be reinterpreted
through spiritual awareness until reality is realized in
consciousness.*

Every question and problem of human experience must
be taken into the depths of consciousness in meditation

---

*For a further discussion of this subject see the chapter, "The New
Horizon," in the author's *The Infinite Way*, © 1947, 1956 by Joel S.
Goldsmith (reprinted 1997 by Acropolis Books, Inc., Lakewood,
CO).

until the intuitive sense has been awakened and has revealed to us the truth of being about which we heretofore have had only an illusory sense or finite concept.

To help you develop a true knowledge of the Christ, take the term, the Christ, into your meditation, beginning with a very humble statement, "I know so little about this, Father; reveal it to me." Close your eyes, and keep your attention centered on the Christ. Every time your mind tries to wander, gently bring it back; bring your thought back; bring your attention back. At the same time your ear is open, and while your ear is attuned and listening, your attention is centered on the Christ. If you will do this, whether it happens the first, second, third, or nineteenth time, ultimately you will catch the vision of the real meaning of the Christ, a meaning that you will never quite be able to explain to anyone else. But you yourself will know it, because the Christ will be an actual presence in your consciousness. It will be a power, an influence, a being, yet It will be something that you cannot define.

You remember that Lao-tze said that if you can define It, It is not that. So it is with the Christ. No matter what you would say about the Christ, it would not quite be It. And so the rest of the knowledge that you would need would have to unfold from within you.

The same thing is true about the word, God. If you have any idea at all that you know what God is, think it over and you will probably discover that you do not really know what God is. True, you may have had little glimpses here and there, but the full and complete unfoldment, or revelation, must come from within, and when that comes, you will be living in an entirely different world from what you are at this moment.

~167~

Take another term, "light." There have been many dedicated souls throughout the ages who could be called, or referred to as, the light of the world–Elijah, Isaiah, Jesus, John, Paul, and many others in more recent years. Whatever you may think you know as to the meaning of the phrase, "the light of the world," there is much more to be known, and this will come to you through taking the word, "light," into your meditation.

One of the deepest mysteries of spiritual wisdom is the Soul. We speak of Soul as God and then we speak of your soul and my soul, but very few know what Soul really means. So take that word, "Soul," and turn to the Father humbly, "Reveal this to me. Give me light on the Soul." Then with the listening ear, that state of receptivity, sooner or later, a day, a week, a month, a year–you will begin to receive impartations, or spiritual awareness, on the subject of Soul.

Illumined and Unillumined Consciousness

The purpose of such meditation is the attainment of illumined consciousness. First, let me explain that the consciousness that thinks of God as something separate and apart from its own being, the consciousness that has not had any teaching along spiritual lines, is what we might term an unillumined consciousness. That is your consciousness or my consciousness before we have received a spiritual teaching. But after we have studied spiritual wisdom for a year or two or three, we learn that God is the reality of being, and then we have taken God out of the skies and identified Him with ourselves.

In our unillumined state of consciousness, we thought of Jesus as Christ, but through illumination we understand

~168~

the Christ to be the Spirit of God, not only of the man, Jesus, ~~but of you and of me~~. For Jesus said, "Before Abraham was, I am.[2]. . . Lo, I am with you alway, even unto the end of the world."[3] If we accept the teaching of Jesus, ~~that makes of the Christ a possibility for every one of us.~~ — *We are called to become like Christ*

In our first few years of metaphysical study, we learned that prayer is not asking God to give us sunny *christ* weather on the day we want to go picnicking, ~~nor is it~~ *died for* ~~asking God to take away our sins~~ or our diseases. When *our sins* we have learned enough to know that prayer is an inner realization of our present spiritual perfection, we have become an illumined consciousness, or at least some degree of illumined consciousness.

Then we come to the point where we learn to take into our meditation any word or term on which we are seeking light or knowledge. We have learned that we do not have to go to a teacher, nor do we have to go to a church. All that we have to do now is to take some particular word or term or idea into our own consciousness and there, in a state of expectancy, wait for the light to shine on it and reveal its meaning to us.

Our friends may say, "Something has happened to you. You have a different look in your eye," or, "You look healthier." But that is the only change they notice. To all appearances we are the same person: We look the same, we feel the same, but actually we are not. The unillumined state of consciousness is being replaced by an illumined state of consciousness. At the same time, nothing has changed in the world. It has not become a better world, but our sense of the world has improved. This world is God's world, ~~and it has always been spiritual and perfect.~~ The illumination that has come to

↳ not after the fall

us does not improve the world: It only improves our concept of the world, our vision of the world, so that we begin to see it more nearly as it really is.

Briefly, that is the difference between an illumined consciousness and an unillumined consciousness. There is nothing of a mysterious nature about it. An illumined consciousness is your consciousness when it has lost some of its erroneous religious or mental teachings, and you have come to the point where you can look out on the world and say, "Why, it's beautiful! And now I realize that it always has been beautiful. The light is within my own vision. Therefore, I am able to see the world through the lighted consciousness, through the illumined consciousness, which I now am." √

That illumined consciousness is the mind that was in Christ Jesus. This mind is no other mind than your own. It is your own mind, but your own mind after it has lost the love of error, the hate of error, and the fear of error. It is not anything mysterious that you contact or get "at-one" with: It is your own mind after it has received some degree of illumination, that is, after you have learned that there is no power outside your own being, and because God is your own being, there is no evil power.

The mind that was in Christ Jesus is the one universal, spiritual mind, infinite and eternal. As you, individually, receive illumination, that which we call your "ignorance" is dispelled, and that mind which was in Christ Jesus is now revealed as your very own mind.

See p. 164

Become a State of Receptivity

When a problem comes to you—your own or that of a patient or friend—turn within, "Father, this problem or person has come to me. Let me have light." Forget the person, forget the problem, and remember that you are not looking for a solution to the problem, but only turning to the Father for light on that subject. The problem is not out in the world: The problem is a belief in your own thought, an ignorance of what God or the Christ is.

In your meditation, you are not seeking somebody's good health, but you are seeking the truth about health, harmony, peace, and joy. Remember, do not dwell on a problem as if you were going to work on it. The problem has been presented to you, but now drop it. When you close your eyes and go within, do not take the person or the problem with you; do not take your ignorance into your meditation. Keep your thought on the light, or the truth, and let that light dawn. Soon you will feel a stirring, that "click," or you will receive a specific answer and you will know that it is done.

Let me return for a moment to my illustration of Lake Erie. As long as I believe that I am Niagara Falls and that that is all there is to me, I keep drawing upon it and using it up, living in, and of, and through Niagara Falls, totally unaware of the abundance of Lake Erie back of me. But through my illumined consciousness, I now learn that Lake Erie is really the substance and the totality and the infinity of Niagara Falls.

Just so, before the light of truth dawned, I believed that the visible me was all there was to me and that I drew on my own mental powers, on my own experience and education. For my strength, I drew on my muscles, on the amount of my sleep, and on the food that I ate; and I tried not to use up more strength than I had taken in as calories and vitamins. But after awakening to my true identity I know that this really is not all of me; it is the least part of me. Back of me is an infinite Ocean called God. I am in, and of, that tremendous Ocean—as a matter of fact, I am that place where the whole Ocean is going to flow *through* and *as*.

Every time we close our eyes in meditation—or keep them open—and open our ear to hear the "still small voice," we place ourselves in a state of receptivity. Each time we do that, we are acknowledging that there is a whole ocean of Intelligence, a whole ocean of Life and Love and Truth, and we are opening our consciousness to that inflow.

Just by opening our ear, we can hear the full voice of God. By opening our consciousness, we have the guidance and direction of God available to us; we have all the health and strength and longevity, immortality, eternality, peace, joy, power, dominion—everything that belongs to God now belongs to us because we have opened our consciousness to Its inflow.

Our existence must be as a state of receptivity, continually opening consciousness and maintaining our consciousness open for It to come through. Do not limit It; do not finitize It; do not think It has to come through a perfect person or through a certain book or through a particular teaching. It may appear to you as a person or as a book, but if you are keeping your mind unlimited and your consciousness open, the book that meets every need for you today may be outmoded tomorrow or the next day or next year, and you may be ready for a whole new book. If you will just keep your consciousness open, there will be a new message, a new flow, continually.

This is true not only of books, but of body. There is no reason why the body should ever lose its vitality and vigor. If it does deteriorate, it is for the same reason that Niagara Falls would ultimately dry up if there were no Lake Erie behind it. If Niagara Falls did not draw upon Lake Erie, it could not last very long. So also, if you and I began using all our knowledge and all our physical strength without drawing upon our Source, we would soon be entirely depleted.

There must come a time when we recognize the truth of Jesus' statement, "Man shall not live by bread alone, but by every word that proceedeth out of the mouth of God."[4] The Word is forever and always proceeding out of the mouth of God, but are we listening, or are we looking in a book to see what it says on some particular page? Over and over again we do that. We limit ourselves to the pages of a book, even a book as all embracing as the Bible, for even the Bible has not said it all—at least it has not said it in as many ways as it can be said, because God, being infinite, must be infinite in expression and God being eternal, must be eternally unfolding.

Do not limit the infinity of God or the eternality of God or the omnipresence of God. God is infinitely, eternally, and omnipresently with you. The only thing that can cut you off from It is closing your consciousness to It.

An Illumined Treatment Never Stops

Many years ago I wrote that a treatment, an illumined treatment, once given, operates throughout the rest of time until its work is done. There is no such thing as a treatment understood ever stopping, because a correct treatment is the word of God. If you ever hear the word of God, rest assured that that word of God will continue to act until your healing takes place, whether you receive the healing that minute, the next day, or the next year.

You do not need a fresh treatment every day. The only reason you need a different treatment or a new one or a special one every day is that what you considered a treatment was not actually a treatment. It was really only your very finite idea of a treatment, probably only some statement of truth, and that is no treatment at all.

A treatment is only complete when you have finished your part of the treatment, listened to the "still small voice," and received an answer. That is a full and complete treatment; that is the word of God made flesh. There is no such thing as the word of God dangling in the air. The word of God must be made flesh; It must dwell among us. Once you receive an answering "click," that treatment will operate in your consciousness until it breaks down the ignorance and reveals an illumined sense of being.

What Did Hinder You?

Spiritual healing is accomplished only when there is no resistance in the healer's thought to the condition or the person. "Agree with thine adversary quickly, whiles thou art in the way with him."[5] In much healing work where use is made of denials and affirmations, there is immediately set up a resistance to error. Remember that the error is not a thing, nor a condition, and it is not a person. So in setting up that resistance, you are almost creating the thing you are resisting.

In spiritual healing, recognize that error does not exist as a reality, no matter in what form it appears—sin, disease, lack, or limitation. When the problem is presented to you, do not resist it, do not deny or affirm it, but take the attitude of "non-resistance," a "divine indifference"—not putting up a mental wall against it, not trying to overcome it, not trying to deny it. Let your attitude be one of freedom from fear, a realization that you do not have to resist a mirage, that you are not going to separate tracks or lift the sky off the mountain.

It is as if Jesus were facing a man with a withered arm and saying, "Stretch forth thine hand."[6] What would make it possible for him to say that to a man with a withered arm, or to the cripple, "Arise, and walk!"[7]? It could only have been because his whole life had been a continuous recognition that there was nothing to hinder this man; there was no presence or power in the arm or leg or in the back that had anything to do with his rising and picking up his bed and walking.

Now, when someone asks you for help, instead of reacting with, "What do I think about this? What do I know? It isn't true; it isn't real"; try to understand what I mean when I tell you to smile because you know that you are being presented with a mirage and that all you have to do is to recognize that it is a mirage. Christ-consciousness does not resist error; It does not recognize error as a power. Jesus told Pilate, "Thou couldest have no power at all against me, except it were given thee from above."[8] You remember that even when walking on the water, Jesus did not accept the law of physics which states that a body of greater density than water must sink.

Spiritual consciousness does not accept in thought the belief of any error existing as a presence or as a power. It looks at any phase or form of error in much the same way as you might look at a moving picture, knowing right well that as soon as the picture is over, the man who has just been shot is going to pick himself up, dust himself off, and get ready to play another part. You sit back, relaxed, knowing all the time that it is just a "movie," and that you are watching the unfoldment of a bit of fiction before your eyes.

In your human experience, you take much the same attitude, not criticizing, judging, condemning, or feeling sorry for the underdog, or for a sick or sinning person, not giving praise to those you think are good, but recognizing all good as coming from God and as having no more reality or power to do anything than the picture on the screen or the mirage on the desert.

When you reach that state of consciousness, in which every call for help arouses in you only the one response, "What can I do about a mirage?" you will begin to see real spiritual healing, Christ-healing, the same type of healing as was done by Jesus and the disciples, healing without taking thought and without the use of a power to overcome any evil. When that state of consciousness is achieved, you are at the place where every call for help rouses in you nothing more and nothing less than a "What can I do about a mirage?"

The Power of Silence

As we go into the higher revelations of the Master, we shall find that it is not necessary to voice thoughts, to use mental might or physical power. We learn that there is within us a divine Presence, an infinite Power, which does much more for us than we can do for ourselves and which operates most effectively in silence. When a practitioner can arrive in his own consciousness at a

place of absolute silence, at a place where he is completely a listening ear, in that flash—it need only last one
blink of an eye—anything that ever was wrong on earth
can be healed.

The silence, the unexpressed thought, the real power,
this tremendous energy, is in that Thing we call the
Christ. We see the effect of It, but never It Itself. No one
can ever see, hear, taste, touch, or smell this infinite
Christ, but we do see Its effects.

Those of you who are gardeners know that when you
plant a seed in the ground, you cannot see the power
that operates through that seed: You can see an effect;
you can see the seed break open; you might even see the
inner part of the seed gradually take root and you may
see something come up from the ground, but you never
see the invisible power producing these changes. That
has never been seen: All that you can see is the effect.

The very power that operates in the silence of the seed
is the power that operates in the silence of our consciousness, and when we attain that degree of silence, we have
attained illumination. As we learn to depend on this
Infinite Invisible, we find things happening in our experience that we had not planned—beautiful things, harmonious and healthful things—and as we become aware of
these experiences, we instinctively recognize them as the
result of this Power, of this unseen Infinite Invisible which
we call the Christ, the presence of God.

We know that that is operating in us and through us
and for us, although at first it is difficult to place a full
reliance on It. It is like that first time when we try to bring
out a healing without relying on some "right" thought or
on some "good" thinking. That first moment, when we
expect to see something happen without taking thought,

is similar to falling into space with nothing to hold one up because there is not a thought to which we can cling.

But in that moment comes the first tangible proof that underneath are the "everlasting arms." When you no longer have a reliance on a person or on a thought, suddenly you begin to feel something as tangible as the "everlasting arms." I wonder if you really know that the "everlasting arms" are an actuality, that there really is such a thing which, even though it cannot be seen or heard, can literally be felt in its invisibility.

In biblical language, I suppose that a complete reliance on the Infinite Invisible is called faith, but in most cases faith is very often a confidence in something that one does not yet know exists. What I am describing is not that sort of thing. It is more like what you would feel if you were in the water with water wings and then said, "I have faith." You have faith because you actually feel those wings and feel the buoyancy of them.

This faith–this understanding and confidence–comes only when you have felt the "everlasting arms." It is not anything you accept before you have felt it. That would only be a faith that it can be, or ought to be, or might be, or should be, or maybe it is in reality. What I mean is that once you have had the first experience of being without the aid of a person or thought, and you have felt Something pick you up, from then on in increasing measure you lean back on that Infinite Invisible.

The Attractive Power of Spirit

In the Infinite Invisible there are ties between us. There is a tie between God, the universal Life and Being, and its individual expression, that which we call individual man and woman. As we become aware of this universal life, we begin to find those who belong to our spiritual demonstration; we begin to find those who are on our level of consciousness. We find those, even though they may never have heard of truth in any form, who may be necessary to our demonstration of the moment. In other words, there is an invisible Force acting on the inner plane attracting to us those people and experiences necessary to our unfoldment. And all this happens without our taking thought, without planning it that way.

We contact the Infinite Invisible when we touch that place in our consciousness which we call God, or the Christ. Even without taking any thought for tomorrow or for the things of tomorrow, we touch the Center which in its infinite and invisible way is really the consciousness of all mankind. It operates on that unseen level to draw to us the harmonies of existence, whether in the form of persons, places, things, circumstances, or conditions.

This activity on the invisible plane is entirely different from working on the visible plane. For example, we all know how to go out and place an advertisement in the newspaper and so attract to ourselves those who have need of what we want to sell. We would know how to go out among our friends and tell them about something we need. We know how to live and move in this outer plane with a fair amount of success.

But what we are going to learn now is how to stop taking thought for the things of life, how to dwell in this Infinite Invisible, and realize that, like the central office of the telephone company, It can connect us with anything anywhere in the world necessary to our unfoldment. The only difference in this case is that we do not have to know the number we want. All we have to do is to be in touch with God, the Center of our being: It knows, It draws, and It contacts—and in ways that seem almost miraculous. If only you could see the operation of this Infinite Invisible! Sometimes it can be seen in meditation, and if you persist, the time will come when you will see the whole secret of life—all that underlies nature, all of the forces of the universe.

Pre-existence

There are people who are on the spiritual path who come to a place where for some reason it seems preferable for them to leave this plane and go on. Because they have been on this path, however, they know better, but at the moment there may be some one problem which they cannot seem to surmount and so they give their consent to going on. Such people, however, are on an ascending scale and their passing is very likely to be a release from materiality because, in that passing, they may have realized the one last thing which they could not quite catch here and in that way be completely set free.

This was the experience of a person I knew who for twenty years or more had studied metaphysics and who had one problem of health that seemed to be more than he could solve. He could not meet it, nor could it be met for him—or at least it was not. Yet here he was, twenty years on the upward path, probably knowing more metaphysics than nine out of ten people, and yet not being quite able to make his demonstration. Finally, he accepted the idea of passing, but within a few hours after the passing, he caught the vision. So much materiality had been done away with that he saw the fullness of the light and was able to give it back to us over here. In a case of this kind, the passing was really a progressive step. Actually, life is not really "over here" or "over there": Life is omnipresent.

When we come to the place where the Infinite Invisible becomes a real part of our existence, when we come to the place where we actually see It operate in our experience—not Its operation, but the effect of Its operation—when each day we have some proof that something is going on in our experience which we cannot account for humanly—something of a good nature—and when we get to the place where we can turn to that Infinite Invisible for guidance, direction, advice, health, and strength, then we come into a state of consciousness which transcends the limitations of time and space.

If you believe that life is immortal and that your life is eternal, you must believe that even should you for any reason at all experience death or passing, that would only be a momentary lapse from consciousness. You would immediately pick yourself up and go right on because consciousness cannot end; consciousness does not stop at the grave. Life does not end at the grave: Life is eternal, and that life manifests itself eternally as what we call our individual experience.

If you accept that as true, you must also accept the truth that life never began. You may think your individual life began in 1900 something, 1890 or 1880 something, but it never did. True, you may have become aware of it at that particular time, and that awareness constitutes your present experience. But as you meditate now, you are going to learn the true meaning of immortality; you are going to learn that long before you became consciously aware of this world, you were alive, living fruitfully and harmoniously just as you will live eternally and immortally after what is called "the passing" from this plane of existence.

Such a knowledge or conviction has deep and tremendous value for us in that it explains many of the human experiences through which we are passing. It reveals to us the spiritual laws that govern human experience, laws which did not begin to operate for us on what we call our birth date, and laws which we will realize as continuing to operate in our experience should we ever consent to the experience of passing.

All this comes under the subject of pre-existence. If our lifework had only to do with learning a little system of healing people, or of postponing the date on their tombstones, none of this would be of too much importance. We would just busy ourselves with learning how to give treatments and thereby bring out a few healings.

Those of you who have been led to the reading of this book and have found your way to the Infinite Way have already begun to leave the state of consciousness where your entire attention is centered on whether you have a few more or a few less dollars, or whether you have a few days more or a few less of pain, to where your interest is in the laws of God. In order fully to understand these laws, you have to begin with the understanding that, because you are these laws and the very activity of these laws, you have never begun and you will never end. Through that understanding you will find your rightful, spiritual place.

Through the Infinite Invisible, all the experiences and persons and books and understanding and knowledge necessary to your unfoldment will be drawn to you. For your human unfoldment you would perhaps look to human ways, but because your unfoldment from now on will be spiritual, even though it appears outwardly as human, you will have to find the answer to it in spiritual law.

The only reason I am discussing immortality and pre-existence is so that when you go into your meditation you do not limit yourself to something you already understand humanly. Turn within and ask for a revelation of the laws of God—those laws which were before Abraham and which will be until the end of the world. You will then begin to understand yourself and your place in God's scheme.

Do any of you believe that you came to earth just to go to school, get married and raise a family, and die? Such a program leaves out the whole idea of God. No matter how happy and how harmonious your human experience may be, could that really be God's plan for His creation? Is not that really too insignificant to credit to Deity? No, turn within and meditate on your individual place in God's plan.

What is God's plan for the spiritual universe? What is God's plan for this world? The only legitimate answer can come from within your own being because it concerns your place in that scheme; it concerns your place in life. Nobody out here in the outer world will ever find his spiritual place unless he has it revealed to him from within, unless he receives from within the impulse that gradually leads him to that place.

~ 12 ~

OPENING CONSCIOUSNESS TO TRUTH

Spiritual healing is a conscious work and cannot be accomplished by sitting around blissfully saying, "Well, let God do it." True, there does come a time when you can legitimately use that expression, but if you were to say it during the early stages of your unfoldment, you would probably be thinking of a God separate and apart from your own being, something outside of you that could do something for you. Such an attitude might cause you to lose your way on the spiritual path through a blind faith.

In healing work, open your consciousness and take the attitude of Samuel, "Speak, Lord; for thy servant heareth."[1] "Be still, and know that I am God"[2]–know that the *I* is pouring Itself forth as individual you.

You can visualize this by once again recalling the illustration of Niagara Falls and Lake Erie. Let us suppose that you are Niagara Falls and, in and of yourself, you are continuously using up yourself so that ultimately there is nothing left. But if you were to realize that behind Niagara Falls there is Lake Erie, and as a matter of fact, actually there is no Niagara Falls–Niagara Falls is only a name given to Lake Erie at one corner of it where it flows over a precipice–there would be no sense of limitation or depletion.

So it is with us. We call ourselves man, but actually we are not: We are that place where God is forever pouring Himself forth as individual you and me. There is really no place where God ends and man begins. That which is visible of us is God—we are God become visible. We are that point where God comes to a focus in an individual, yet infinite manner. There is no place where man and God can be separated and where you can say that here is man and there is God, any more than you can say that up to a certain point there is a Lake Erie and from that point on there is a Niagara Falls. Niagara Falls and Lake Erie are not two but one, and all that Lake Erie is, Niagara is; all that Lake Erie has, Niagara has; but Lake Erie is continuously pouring itself forth as Niagara Falls. There is no place in the whole watershed where you can separate the one from the other.

Since it is true that all of the Godhead is pouring Itself forth as individual you and me, the only reason for any lack in our experience—whether it is lack of health or lack of wealth or opportunity or a lack in any form—is that we have come to believe that what we see is all there is of us, that this visible form is our being; instead of which, we merely are that place through which all of God is pouring forth.

To correct that mistake and overcome that belief of separation, one thing and one thing alone is necessary: Our consciousness must be kept open at all times for the flow, for God to flow out as you or as me.

Open consciousness is the realization that God is pouring Himself forth as you and as me and that there is no place where God ends and you or I begin. It is all one never ending flow, but this flow must be maintained as a continuous thing.

Morning, noon, and night—especially after we get into bed at night and before we get out of bed in the morning, and then as many hours throughout the day as possible—we should remember, "I and my Father are one,"[3] and that this Father is pouring Himself forth as individual being. Even if we do not sit down to meditate, we should, for a second or a minute, open our consciousness to the realization of this relationship between God, the Infinite Invisible, and ourselves, the visible manifestation of that Infinite Invisible.

"Thou wilt keep him in perfect peace, whose mind is stayed on thee,"[4] and from now throughout the rest of time we are going to keep our consciousness stayed on God, every hour opening our ears or just looking up toward the skies. This will be our recognition of the infinitude of God pouring forth as individual being. After a month of such practice, we may look in our mirror and not recognize ourselves.

As you sit in meditation, you will notice a change taking place in your system: Your breathing slows down; your thoughts race less and less and finally cease; and you may find that your diaphragm will go in and your chest come out because that is probably the normal position of the body; but whether it is or not, it brings a beautiful sense of peace with it.

The rhythm of the universe is taking possession of you. You may not move, but you feel that you are in tune; you feel a rhythm; you feel that there is a harmony of being and a mental peace. But it is more than a mental peace: It is a spiritual peace which settles upon you, and you can sit for many, many minutes in that attitude. You rest back in peace and harmony, but at the same time become receptive to impartations from within. You will find many passages in the Bible describing that beautiful peace that comes when you feel that you are held in the "everlasting arms," when the Soul is at rest and the Soul-senses quiet.

Do not let this become an attitude of mental laziness, stagnation, or of falling asleep, however, because what I am describing is the direct opposite of that. What I am describing is a spirit of alertness in which you do no thinking. It is a quickening alertness, yet carrying with it the feeling of the "peace that passeth understanding," the joy of being, without any apparent or external reason for that joy. It is an inner attunement.

"Resist Not Evil"

Ultimately, all your healing work will be done in that way, and you will come to the place where you will not think a single thought when you sit down to help anyone or even to help yourself. You will sit back and become quiet; you may remind yourself that there is no place where Lake Erie ends and Niagara Falls begins, that is, no place where God ends and man begins. All of the Godhead is pouring forth as you; all that the Father has is yours; all the wisdom, all the knowledge, all that you need to know is omnipresent as your very own consciousness.

With a few little reminders such as, "'Speak, Lord; for thy servant heareth'; here I am waiting for the 'still small voice,'" you stay in that peace until the "click" comes, and then the treatment is complete. You will know that the patient has either had a healing or has felt a great sense of relief or freedom, or that the situation has been met in some way.

If you find it necessary to repeat the treatment over and over again, the same procedure is followed—finding the center of your being, finding your oneness with the Eternal, feeling the complete rhythm of this universe and keeping yourself in tune with it. There is a spiritual law underlying such meditation in which no thought takes place, no argument or treatment, just the conscious awareness of God's presence and that sense of peace. Its basis is in that law, "Resist not evil," one of the most powerful laws to be found in the entire Bible. What it is really saying is that error is not real, and if you resist it, you make it real, and the battle is on.

We are always being told how to protect ourselves from evil, what to do about it when we meet up with it, while all the time it is but a mental image. "Resist not evil." When someone calls for help, do not put up a mental barrier and deny evil. In the face of any errone-ous picture or discord, instead of denying it, instead of saying it is not real when to all appearances it is actually taking place in the outer picture, do not argue, do not fight it, do not resist it at all, but just sit back and say, "I wonder how real you can be?"

Instead of denying the error, let your spiritual sense reinterpret the scene. Let God reinterpret whatever the picture is before you:

Since I am infinite Consciousness and include within my own being the entire universe, through my consciousness of this truth, I become the law unto that universe. I accept in my consciousness the revelation that evil is unreal, and therefore does not have to be resisted or battled; I become a law unto my universe through my conscious realization of the spiritual laws of life.

I see all injustice, all lack of integrity, all inharmony, all discord, all lack of cooperative action as merely the finite

~189~

interpretation of That which is real and therefore I do not battle them: I sit back quietly at peace. I "resist not evil," and thereby become the law to that situation and watch it automatically dissolve.

Then, and then only, can you say, "It really is not real, and I have seen its unreality demonstrated and the reality made manifest."

If you fight and battle evil, you make it a reality and give it a power that may make it impossible for you ever to overcome it. If you resist anyone who wrongs you, you set up an antagonism within your consciousness and even if that particular person did not harm you, some other one might come along who would, because you have made that antagonism so real to you that it now has to be battled and overcome.

If you stand on your human rights, even on your legal rights, you may find yourself engaged in a battle. Your work is not to battle, but to stand still and see the salvation of the truth that God is all that is ever appearing in circumstance or condition. Until you learn to do that, whatever you are beholding, even when it is good, represents your finite sense of what really is. So remember that "resist not evil" is the acme of spiritual healing. It enables you to face any situation in the world with a disdainful, "So what?"

Let God Interpret the Scene

In spiritual healing, there is no mental action, there is no conscious thought-taking, there is no conscious affirming or denying. Rather is there the conviction that inasmuch as the reality of the picture presented to you is in and of God, you are going to let God interpret it to you.

Even when you are reading a book, reading the Bible, or listening to a lecture or to a teacher, sit back with the feeling, "I am not so much interested in the words I am reading or hearing as in how God is going to interpret them to me." Let your state of receptivity take in what is being said or read; let the Infinite within you translate it for you.

It is foolish for anyone to sit and look at a sinful or diseased person and say, "You are God's perfect image." That is really stretching it a little too far! But it is quite another thing to turn within and ask God, "How about interpreting this for me and letting me see it as it is?"

In asking God to interpret the scene, there is no resistance, no acknowledgment that there is an error to be overcome, no acknowledgment that there is a sinner to be reformed, no acknowledgment that there is a lack or limitation that must be met—only the conviction that here is something you do not understand any more than you would if somebody were talking in Sanskrit and you could only understand the meaning of the hodge-podge of words which were being poured into your conscious-ness through an interpreter versed in that language. So you must let God interpret this scene with which you are being presented in the language of Spirit.

Since our premise is that all action is mind-action and that mind is the instrument of God, everything that is appearing to us is the activity of God. So what we are doing now is not overcoming error, but rightly interpret-ing the picture before us. Evil is not a thing or a person: It is a misinterpretation of some activity of God because God is literally all. Since there is no action apart from mind-action and since there is no activity apart from eternal life, even in looking at what the world calls death, we are actually witnessing eternal life in action.

That is the only reason Jesus could raise anyone from the dead. That is the only way a practitioner can bring the dying back to life, not by saying, "You are dying, and I am going to bring you back to life," but by recognizing that there is nothing going on but the activity of God, interpreting Itself through the mind. The practitioner must sit in peace and quiet until God, the inner Interpreter of his being, interprets the scene for him. The practitioner never does the interpreting.

Avoid the Use of Metaphysical Clichés

The response of some metaphysical workers is at times very annoying to the serious student of spiritual wisdom. Why does anyone ever say, "It isn't true," or, "It isn't real"? All this is nonsense. Why does anyone say it if he believes that it isn't true? The fact of the matter is that he believes that it is true or he would not be saying that it isn't.

I have never known of a millionaire who went around saying, "I'm rich and I know it!" That is usually done by the person who is not rich and who is trying to hypnotize himself into the belief that he is. You do not find many healthy people going around saying, "I am well; I am God's perfect child"; and you do not find satisfactorily employed people saying, "God is my employer." No, they have such a consciousness of supply and health that it is not necessary for them to go around bolstering their morale by means of statements which they hope to make come true.

When you are faced with what appears to your sense to be evil, be honest about it and recognize that it is a nasty looking picture, one which you do not like. You will find that you have a great deal more respect for yourself when you make statements that you yourself believe, instead of going around making empty denials which in the back of your mind you do not really believe, but only wish were true. This habit of making statements, affirming and denying, has served many as stepping stones, but for some it has been a stepping stone to the grave, to an institution, or to an accident. For those who have been wise enough to see that it was just a temporary stage from which they would emerge, it really was a stepping stone into a higher consciousness.

In this field, as in everything else, we are face to face with the fact that the average person is not an independent thinker. He is much more apt to be like a piece of blotting paper, willing to absorb what somebody says or writes. For that reason you will hear students make all manner of ridiculous statements, some of which they have heard from others and some of which can be found in print.

Let us resolve to be honest at least: "I will no longer go around saying I am rich if I am hungry, or well if I am sick. From now on, I will make the open admission that I feel terrible and I am hungry, but I know right well there is a right interpretation to this thing. There is a right answer, and I am going to sit down and meditate and let God get me back on the beam."

If you catch the idea that even that which is appearing to be discord is some part of God's allness because the activity of God is all there is, it is perfectly all right to assure or reassure yourself with, "Wait! I don't have to believe this picture, since I do know that in the nature of

Reality all is good. So now let me sit back and realize it. Let me receive the divine impartation that will dispel this illusion."

Behold the World Through the Soul-Senses

Let me tell you one great truth: No amount of mental work is going to heal your disease or your lack. You might as well make up your mind right here and now that mental power is not Christ-power. Christ-power is gentleness and peace, an all-knowing confidence and understanding. It has nothing to do with fighting. There is no need for all this mental battling.

You who are reading this book are doing so because perhaps you are ready to give up at least some of your reliance on mental processes. Some divine urge within your own being has brought this message to you, and you would not be reading it were you not ready. Even while you are rereading passages and finding helpful statements to buoy you up at times, remember that these are just temporary stopgaps, reminding you to sit back and let God, the infinite Intelligence of your being, interpret whatever needs interpreting.

The earth is really heaven, but heaven seen through finite sense, "through a glass, darkly," and inasmuch as with your eyes you will never see it any other way, why not acknowledge that and sit back with your eyes closed, letting your spiritual sense reveal the harmony of being to you?

The statement that God is all is not what brings out a demonstration. There must be the development of the spiritual sense, what I call the Soul-sense, so that you perceive that which is not visible or tangible to the physical senses. You perceive it through your inner Soul-sense. You catch a glimpse of that when you have developed the faculty of discernment. For example, in your reading, you have no difficulty then in recognizing the difference between a statement that comes out of a consciousness of truth and one that is someone's human opinion, with no consciousness of truth behind it. Something within you does that, and that something is your Soul-sense.

Remember that the senses of hearing, sight, taste, touch, and smell are our concepts of the spiritual activity of Consciousness, and therefore, the five physical senses represent our concept of the real Soul-faculties. If we did not all have a measure of developed Soul-faculty, not one of us would spend time on spiritual subjects because to material sense it would seem to be a waste of time. To us it is not a waste of time: It is an investment! It is our measure of spiritual sense that makes it possible for us to pursue the study of spiritual wisdom with unflagging devotion. Our intellect would rebel at this; therefore, some measure of developed spiritual sense is requisite for a person to be able to hold his attention on spiritual subjects for any length of time. The measure of our Soul-sense, or spiritual sense, must be increased, and that can be done by letting God translate any and every appearance into its spiritual significance.

Dealing with Premonitions

When, as sometimes happens, we have fore-vision, foresight, or are able to catch a glimpse of some scene or event which has not happened, but which happens the next day or month, we know that inasmuch as we are recognizing God as the only activity, what is coming to us is the misinterpretation of the activity of divine Wisdom, and so we must understand that this is only the finite, human sense of some spiritual activity. Then, in that realization, we can let the divine mind reinterpret that vision.

There was a time when I did not know how to do this, and I had some very unpleasant experiences.

When I was just a youngster, my father was a European traveler and spent much of his time abroad. One day, I went to my mother and said, "Mom, something is wrong in Europe; something is wrong with Pop!" There was nothing we could do about this premonition because all we knew was that Father had just landed in England. But the next day we had a cable from him that he had been on his way to catch the Nottingham express and for the first time in 100 trips he had missed his train. That was the very day the Nottingham express was wrecked and everyone aboard killed—101 people. However, my premonition had nothing to do with the fact that my father missed his train because I had not yet learned what to do about such forewarnings.

There were other experiences of warnings of impending danger, as for example, when I astonished my mother by telling her of a railroad wreck in Connecticut, although neither one of us had any way of knowing whether or not this had happened until it was verified in the paper that night. Later on I often caught a certain signal when someone I knew, someone in the family or a close friend, was about to pass on. I never knew or understood these experiences, nor did I know what to do about them.

Later I learned how to reinterpret these things and thereby reverse them, and when the signal came, to prevent their happening. This occurred once in the

Middle West when a woman in a department store came up to the buyer with whom I was talking and asked to be introduced to me. She told me that a member of my family would die that week either from heart disease or from an automobile accident.

At that time I was a student of Christian Science, so I got busy right there and then in the realization that God was the only presence and the only power and that the only activity that could take place was the activity of mind, and that this prophecy was merely the same as any negative appearance of sin or disease, the reverse of that which was actually happening.

A few days later a member of my family was in an automobile which went up into the air on two wheels and then settled back on all four again. That was the end of that. There was no death that time.

Soon afterwards, I was in the healing practice and found that every time some patient was in danger, I got that same signal, but by then I had learned how to reinterpret these premonitions. I knew that all such pictures were misinterpretations of divine activity. You, too, must realize that no picture appears before you except that picture which is painted by the hand of the Divine, and that picture is always good. Whatever picture is appearing is merely the misinterpretation of that divine activity. Continue your work until you get the feeling that comes when a healing takes place.

Reinterpret Every Human Picture

Deal with a good picture in the same way. You want only Divinity Itself. Otherwise, if you were a practitioner, all you would want would be that your patient become well. Physical health is not the object of our work. When a patient says, "I have no fever," or, "My body seems all right," even then our work is to realize that the appearance of physical health is only a misinterpretation of the divine health which is life eternal. Every human picture is mesmeric suggestion; every human picture is a finite presentation of the Infinite—even the good ones. Every human picture!

The end and object of our work is not to make sick people well through any kind of a process. The end and object of our work is to reverse the whole human picture so that we can see it as it divinely is—eternal and immortal. Whatever the picture presented to the sight, good or bad, immediately there should be the recognition that God is the author and the creator, that it is infinitely good, and that whatever is appearing finitely is but the false interpretation of that infinite, beautiful picture which cannot be seen with the physical eyes, but which can be felt with the spiritual senses.

This is very important because on this one point the Infinite Way goes far beyond most metaphysical practice: It goes beyond merely making unemployed people employed, demonstrating money for them, or demonstrating a perfect heart for them: It goes into the realm of bringing to light the spiritual selfhood of the individual, which is unchanging and undying.

What I am trying to tell you is not to believe what your eyes see, even if the picture is a good one. Whatever it is, it is always only a finite interpretation of the infinite real which is waiting to be spiritually discerned and realized with your spiritual senses.

We are not to be satisfied even with good human pictures because "My kingdom is not of this world."[5] We are not to be satisfied with materiality–physical health, material wealth, or human companionship–but we should immediately translate and reinterpret every picture that comes to us.

If we are continually reversing the picture, whatever it is–good, bad, or indifferent–knowing that all good is the infinite good of God individualizing itself in our experience, then we have nothing to fear, and those human beings whom we have trusted as friends will not turn on us and rend us.

The essence of the teaching of the Infinite Way is that we are not to be satisfied with good human beings or with human goodness. Let us not be engaged in a ministry of making sick people well or poor people rich. We have been chosen to do our work on a higher plane than that. "Ye have not chosen me, but I have chosen you."[6]

Consciousness has reached out to us and said, "You are ready for the higher step."

~ 13 ~

MYSTICISM

The true meaning of mysticism is any philosophy or religion that teaches oneness with God. Mysticism reveals the possibility of receiving impartations or guidance directly from God, of communing with God, of being consciously at-one with God, and receiving good from God without any intermediary. And so the teaching of the Infinite Way is a mystical one because, above all things, its purpose is to achieve oneness with God.

One of the highest mystical statements of which I have any knowledge, one which will provide you with a passkey to heaven, a key to harmony of mind, body, and business, health and wealth and all other things is: Your oneness with God constitutes your oneness with all spiritual being and things.

This you will find in my writings, but you will also find that it has not been taken too seriously by most of those who have read it. Except in a few cases, it has not been recognized as one of the supreme wisdoms of the world, possibly because, in the first place, it is not stated in mystical or cryptic language, but in plain English, and secondly, because most people have not formed the habit of analyzing statements.

Our Oneness with God Appears as Form

My oneness with God constitutes my oneness with all spiritual being and things. Go back to the illustration of the telephone. You cannot get a telephone number any-where in the world without first going through the central office, but once you have contacted the central office, you can reach any place on the face of the globe that has a telephone. So it is that if you contact God, if you have a conscious realization of God, if you become consciously one with God, then automatically and instantaneously you are at one with the entire universe of spiritual being and idea.

Everything that you see, hear, taste, touch, or smell is but a finite concept of a divine idea. For example, an automobile is a vehicle for transportation which will wear out or become obsolete and require another investment to replace it. But behind the idea, or object, of automobile is the divine idea of transportation, and transportation is really a spiritual activity; it is an activity of mind imparting itself as idea to individual being. Therefore, if you once contact God, or Spirit, you have contacted the spiritual law of transportation, and if your need for an automobile is a real one, you will be sur-prised how quickly you will obtain it. A seat in an airplane, a steamship ticket, or anything pertaining to transportation would immediately be available to you because of your oneness with the infinite Source of all good.

This does not mean that anyone should attempt to demonstrate an automobile. But suppose that I am in San Francisco and my home is in Los Angeles, and in a human sense I must bridge that four hundred odd miles. I have need of transportation, and apparently there is no immediate solution to the problem. So I sit down and realize my oneness with God. I realize my oneness in as many different ways as I can: I may think of the wave as being one with the ocean, or of the sunbeam as one with the sun, or of the Selfhood that is one with God. In any way that I can, I relate myself to God until finally I come into the realization: *All that the Father has is mine because we are one. There is no separation between God and man; God and man are one. I and the Father are one; all that the Father has is right here where I am.*

If I can achieve that realization, if I can obtain that inner sense of peace that we call "the click," very quickly I will find that my transportation to Los Angeles appears. It may be an invitation to ride with someone; it may be a railroad ticket; it may be someone down there sending for me. It could appear in any way, but I would not at any time have to think about transportation: I would only have to think about my oneness with God and about the immediate availability of God in every form.

Much the same thing can happen if there is a need for a home, whether in your present community or a different one. Again, you do not use this truth to demonstrate a house or a place in which to live; but if this truth does not, or cannot, bring fulfillment and harmony, it would not be the truth of being, because Jesus said, "I am come that they might have life, and that they might have it more abundantly"[1]–*I* am come that ye might be fulfilled. Certainly a home and companionship are part of your fulfillment. Having arrived at a place where you know that you have a need for a home, now forget the home, turn within, and realize God. Realize that the only home there is, is in your own consciousness; realize that you live and move and have your being in God, in true Consciousness. True Consciousness is omnipresent as your own being. As you realize the true nature of home, embracing all the spiritual qualities of God, such as protection, love, joy, beauty, cooperativeness, safety, and security, your home will appear. Conscious oneness with God is what brings it into manifestation–not going outside to demonstrate things.

Remember always that the basis of our work is: "Seek ye first the kingdom of God."[2] One of the ways of seeking first the kingdom of God is this realization of oneness because, when you have demonstrated your conscious oneness with God, all the *things* are added unto you. Therefore, oneness with God constitutes oneness with every spiritual being and idea.

It may be that some person is needed to bring about the happy adjustment of your affairs–the right real estate agent, the right banker, the right investment counselor, or the right metaphysical teacher. The right one would not be contacted by simply desiring the right one, but by consciously realizing your oneness with God.

Your Consciousness Unfolds as Truth

It is the same when a person is seeking truth. What such a person wants is the highest unfoldment that there is for his particular state of consciousness, the unfoldment which will meet his particular needs. Each one may use a different avenue to arrive at his goal, but perhaps for most seekers, the public libraries with their thousands of books offer the easiest, quickest, and most accessible way of investigating different approaches to truth.

However, you might read all but one of those books and not find what you are seeking, and all that time spent in reading might be time wasted. It would have been just as easy to go to the center of your own being and there realize that God and Truth are synonymous; and inasmuch as you are one with God, you are one with Truth, and therefore all the Truth in the universe is available to you now—not available tomorrow, but now—available right here where you are. There is no time, place, or space which can separate you from Truth, from all the Truth in the universe because you cannot be separated from God.

As you meditated in that way, day in and day out, you would be led to the one book that really would open up the floodgates for you. From there on, you would be led from book to book, teacher to teacher, but only to those that were in accord with your own consciousness or those that would meet your particular need. It is not necessary to read every book in the world in order to find the truth you need. You can be led to those authors and teachers and those Scriptures that are in harmony with your particular state of consciousness.

I wish sometimes that the spiritual teachers of the Western World could follow the practice of the Hindu swamis in India whose students come and live with them for three years. Then at three o'clock in the morning, if the swami feels the flash of the Spirit, he sends word for them to come at once. When they meet, the swami talks and talks—perhaps until five o'clock—and then they go back to bed. If at seven o'clock the swami feels that he is ready to talk again, out come the students at seven o'clock. They never know at what hour of the day or night they are going to be summoned into the presence of their teacher to hear the pearls of divine wisdom that flow through him from God.

There are moments in the experience of every spiritual teacher when true wisdom pours forth. It was in one such moment when I seemed to be afire with the Spirit that this lesson on mysticism was revealed to me: Inasmuch as I am consciously one with God, I must be consciously one with the individual consciousness of everyone. Certainly all those who are a part of my consciousness must be receiving the same message I am receiving. As this truth kept pouring and pouring itself through me, I longed to be able to share it with my students all over the world, and so powerful was this revelation that I would not have been at all surprised had some of them written that they received the same message at the same time.

Those of us who follow the mystical path will ultimately learn that it is not really necessary to use words to reveal spiritual wisdom. All of us can receive the messages and impartations necessary to our unfoldment from the divine Wisdom within because they are not dependent upon human contact.

Activity, the Divine Idea Unfolding

In the mystical approach, you realize that, whether it is metaphysical teaching or healing, selling refrigerators or real estate, or inventing a new egg beater or a new process for refining oil, every right activity of human experience is the divine idea unfolding. It is really the activity and operation of universal Intelligence that does it all. It takes place as the activity of this divine Intelligence and Wisdom, which interprets Itself through the instrument of the mind. Because that Intelligence is your intelligence and mine, It is automatically interpreting Itself through the mind of everyone concerned at the same time. That eliminates the necessity of advertising a product or a teaching, because the very moment an idea is implanted in what I call my individual being, it is automatically implanted in your consciousness; but if you have not been trained to bring it forth out of your own consciousness, you may have to read books, study, or go to a teacher in order to have it unveiled for you.

You must know that what you are reading in this book is already a part of your consciousness. If it were not, you could not understand it because it would be as if I were writing in Sanskrit. However, if you were at that level of consciousness where Sanskrit was a necessity, you would be led to that person who could teach it to you.

Nobody can ever give you anything that is not already a part of your consciousness. Therefore, the writer is not giving you anything: He is but unveiling it for you. It is all within your own consciousness, and if you had not found this book, you would have found another one or would have heard it in your sleep or even as you were walking along the street. In other words, if this message were dependent upon a person or a book, where would God be in that picture? No, every person in this world who is ready for this message is receiving it this minute.

Conscious Oneness with God Is Oneness With All Spiritual Being and Idea

This is the miracle of mysticism. Your conscious oneness with God makes everything in this world available the moment that you need it. Nobody can keep it away from you, either—nobody. But this is only true if you are following the spiritual path. Conscious oneness with God is mysticism. *Conscious oneness with God constitutes your oneness with all spiritual being and with every spiritual idea.*

For example, money is just a human concept, but it is a human concept of a divine idea, representing love, gratitude, sharing, and cooperation; it is a spiritual idea which cannot *come* to you, because it already is an embodied idea and activity of your consciousness. When you feel pressed for money, one of the reasons is that you are looking for it from some source outside yourself, when all the time it is hidden within your own consciousness. It is already within you, but you are looking for it in a person, place, or thing.

In the many, many stories told of the search for the Holy Grail, for that gold cup from which Jesus is supposed to have drunk at the Crucifixion, the seekers always came home, impoverished and broken in health, dropping wearily and despondently at their own door. In every version, is told the story of the person who gives his whole life and fortune to the search in the outer world only to find the long sought for treasure on his return home: He finds it in his garden, perhaps hanging to the branch of a tree; he reaches forth his hand at his own table, and it appears.

The story of the Holy Grail is symbolic of the treasure hidden within our consciousness, within our own being, there by virtue of our oneness with God. That is only another way of stating: *My oneness with God constitutes my oneness with all spiritual being and with every spiritual idea or thing.* To me that represents one of the highest statements of spiritual truth. It is in my writings in just that simple language, so simple and direct that sometimes people do not recognize it as "the pearl of great price." This statement: *'My oneness with God constitutes my oneness with all spiritual being and with every spiritual idea or thing,'* ranks as one of the highest statements of truth, one which will bring you nearer the realization of heaven on earth than any other.

Realization on the Inner Plane Appears as Fulfillment on the Outer

The very highest mystical statement of truth that I know is, "My kingdom is not of this world."[3] I doubt that Jesus ever said anything of a more mystical nature than that. He could say later, "I have overcome the world,"[4] because of his realization that "My kingdom is not of this world." That statement immediately sets us free from the desire for person, place, thing, circumstance, or condition. It sets us free from the world of effects and makes it possible for us to live in conscious union with Cause, with God.

If we were to demonstrate effects by the millions, we still would be dealing with something that could turn to dust in our hands. But if once we achieve conscious union with Cause, or God, then we have no further interest in the things of this world except to enjoy them as they come along. We then are still in the world, but not of it. I, myself, find pleasure in many of the beautiful and enjoyable things of this world, but there is no longer an engrossing attachment to them.

There is no such thing as a time or a place wherein we would have less than the fullness of the kingdom, if once we obtained the consciousness that "My kingdom is not of this world." But we must ever be on the alert not to become bound up in the things of the world. Do not be concerned about "this world"—this is the mystical path. Do not be concerned about the flesh—this is the way of the Spirit. Do not be too concerned about the solution to any problem—the problem is only temporary.

Be concerned with the inner plane of being. It is on the inner plane that we make our contact with God. On the outer, we behold humanly the fruitage of the work on the inner plane. It is possible, of course, for a person to make his contact with God on the inner plane, as many ascetics do, many who retire from the world and live in monasteries and convents; it is possible to make that contact on the inner plane and absolutely drop the whole outer world and experience a joyous inner life. But for most of us in the Western World that does not seem quite natural or right, except for the few who attain such heights on the inner plane that they can do more for humanity in that way than by being a part of the world.

For the most of us, however, what we learn on the inner plane can prove to be the greatest blessing to those in the outer world. Therefore until such time as the call comes to leave the world, we should live in it. We should share with those of this world all the depths that are being plumbed in our inner life.

On the inner plane, that is, within our own being, is where we touch God, where we touch the spiritual identity of everything that appears as person, place, or thing. Touching the Reality within makes it manifest to us in the outer—as family, friends, students, patients, activities, or even as books to read. It is a strange thing that every time I touch some new note within, somebody either gives me a book or recommends one that takes me just a step further or corroborates some point I have already discovered on the inner plane. Furthermore, every time I touch a new sense within, it appears outwardly as some new friend, some new helper, or some kind of new activity.

Regardless of the particular activity in which you may be engaged, contact God within yourself and trust that contact to bring to you all that is necessary for your unfoldment. It may not come the day you expect it. As a matter of fact, it may have to come all the way from China. Give it a chance to get here. Moreover, the person necessary to the solution of your problem may not be in a position just at the moment to become a party to the demonstration.

Do not set time limits upon your demonstration. Find the kingdom of God within your own being, make that contact, and understand that now you are depending for your outer expression on your inner demonstration. You must first make it on the inner plane, and then the outer plane will take care of itself.

I keep repeating to you that the mystical life is one in which you are completely independent of person, thing, or activity on the human level. Yet it is one in which you are never separated from person, place, thing, or activity, but where the whole solution is consummated within your own being through your contact with God and is then brought into visibility as if there were an unseen hand manipulating all the strings.

Students of the Infinite Way are not just metaphysicians who have found some truth they believe will enable them to hornswoggle God into doing their will, nor have they found some secret means of getting from God what could not be obtained in any other way. They are not spending their time making affirmations or denials, but living in conscious realization of God, making God as much a part of their conscious life as Jesus did, insofar as they can.

The Mystical Path Demands a Sacrifice of Self

There are spiritual demands made on every one of us. For example, there is a spiritual demand made on me to live so as to present a clear and clean consciousness to the world, one devoid of self-interest and deception, one devoid of anything that would separate this message from its Source. God is both the creator and the teacher of this message, and all those to whom He has entrusted it have an obligation and responsibility to present that message in its purity and its entirety.

It takes clear thinking and clean living to be the right kind of teacher: It requires honesty of purpose, it requires dedication; it requires more than a mere intellectual knowledge of truth. It is true that now that the letter of this message has been set forth in print in many books, anybody could attempt to teach it. I doubt very much, however, whether any student would benefit greatly by such teaching unless behind it there is spiritual integrity. The words of themselves will not lift anybody's consciousness. The words of themselves will not convey the spirit of truth. The pages are just so much more black print added to the bookshelves in the world.

It takes the consciousness of an inspired individual, one aflame with love for God, to impart spiritual truth. Spiritual teaching not only requires a consecrated teacher, but also, as students, people who are willing to sacrifice time, money, or pleasure in the pursuit of truth, people who are eager to sit at the feet of the Master.

And what is the Master? The Master is not a man! The Master is this divine message, this truth. That is the Master! And to sit at Its feet means really to cleanse your consciousness of all self-will, selfish desire, really to lay your all on the altar of this Truth in real surrender, "Everything I have of a material nature—all of it added together—is not worth even one drop of spiritual truth." In such a purified state of consciousness, you would be able to receive and assimilate and respond to the truth of being.

How many times has Jesus told us that we must leave all for the Christ? How many times has he pointed out the multitudinous excuses given: This person had to bury his father-in-law; this one had to get married; and this one had to pick his donkey up out of a ditch. How many have been invited to the feast—and could not come? Too many other things to do! Too many other obligations! But to receive the divine Light means to offer one's self on the altar of spiritual truth. It means to sacrifice all sense of self—all sense of selfishness or desire for personal gain.

Actually, there is no need to strive for personal gain because spiritual truth blesses one and all alike. The more you give, the more you have. So it is, whether one is at the moment teaching and imparting spiritual truth or whether one is temporarily the student, the more he gives, the more he will receive. I have never yet spoken or written a word which did not lift me higher, because what I speak or write does not come out of my human intellect. It is not something that I have made up. It is an impartation that comes from me at the moment that I speak and it means just as much to me as to those who hear it, perhaps more, because I can best appreciate it, knowing the depths out of which it comes. I know the nights of wakefulness and the pain often required to bring through deep truth.

Trials on the Spiritual Path

This I must tell you, too: The spiritual path is not one of roses without thorns. When you decide to make the transition into the mystical life, you will find that it is necessary to give up many of your former concepts of body, business, and pleasure. You will find new experiences awaiting you, and in that period of transition, it is not all harmony, "because strait is the gate, and narrow is the way, which leadeth unto life, and few there be that find it."[5] This path is not easy in its early stages. As a matter of fact, learning these lessons may prove to be very painful because many of them come only through deep suffering. Strange, but without that suffering, we perhaps would not learn them because when all is well and we are at peace with the world, we do not really make an effort or really try deep down within ourselves.

We frequently go along thinking how well everything is going—and there is no progress. It is the depth of our trials and tribulations that forces us up, and often the person who has suffered most, attains the most—not because this is necessary or because there is any God decreeing it, but because of inertia, because of our desire to continue along the way in which we are going and at the speed we are going, because we like to know that each day is going to be followed by another day of no pain and no lack and no limitation.

I have read the lives of many who have gone far on the spiritual path, and as yet I have not found any one of them who has not had his Gethsemane. These great truths are not easy of attainment. If the trials do not come in one form, they come in another. Jesus faced trials, many of them, and while it is true that we do not have to go through persecution or withstand public condemnation, we do experience a measure of personal strife. It may be within our family. It may be within our community. Somewhere, somehow, or in some way, if we are to plumb the depths of spiritual wisdom, each one of us must go through a period of transition.

One of the greatest of trials may come when you begin to stop depending on persons or when you stop sending out bills to your patients and decide that you are going to depend solely on the Christ. That first month when the adjustment is taking place and you cannot ask anybody for money, nor can you send out a bill, is a period when you sometimes quake a little and wonder if this dependence on the Christ is going to work. Then when you come to that great place of healing without using words or thoughts in treatment, never doubt but that you have a trial, a "River Jordan" to cross. First comes the temptation, "I don't think I am doing justice to my patients; I don't feel that I am working hard enough"; and then comes the second temptation, after some beautiful healings have taken place and the patients have been very generous, and you feel, "I can't take this money; I didn't really work for it; I didn't do enough to earn this."

There are all kinds of trials that come with this life. When you arrive at that place where your response to a call for help is as simple as, "I really believe that God is the life of all being; and therefore, any appearance of error must be nothing more nor less than a hallucination, a temptation, coming to me to believe in a selfhood apart from God. I refuse to believe it," and are satisfied to let that be the treatment; then when you remember the earlier forms of treatment you had used there comes that period of hesitation and doubt. Such a period of transition is not easy. There comes a time when the members of your family begin to say that you must have gone crazy, and the members of your church tell you, "Well, you certainly have gone off the beam now."

In one way or another, trials come to us, either through our own selves, through our family, or our patients. There may even come for a time serious problems of health and supply—either our own or our patients—but we have to learn to stand fast, we have to learn to sit up nights with them. We have to learn to go away for "forty days" too, even though it is not an actual forty days, but only a figurative one. It is going away into the "closet," into our sanctuary, and just praying our old heart out, "Let this cup pass from me—but if it doesn't, I can take that too."

All these things come to us on this way—the straight and narrow. Once you have given up your reliance on all human means of salvation, once you have chosen this way, you will find how straight and narrow it is. You find how few there be who go in thereat and for awhile it will almost seem as though you are cut off from all friendship; it will seem that nobody in the world understands you and that you will never meet anyone who can. I know, because for many years, not only did I not have the opportunity to speak this way in public, but I did not even have the opportunity to speak of these things in private. I had to be silent because the moment I attempted to express any of these ideas, people would misunderstand.

If your reliance is on the inner plane, if your reliance is on your contact with God, and you feel yourself cut off from dependence on human means of demonstrating your good, there comes a period when you have to sit quietly and secretly within your own being. You have to work this out without telling the outside world about it. You have to prove it, and when you have done this, the evidence is so great that you do not have to tell it any more except when you are in the process of teaching. You never have to tell anyone that you have found "the pearl of great price." In the first place, if you told it, it would almost be proof positive that you had not found it. It is not necessary to talk about it because your whole life, your whole attitude, and your whole being are evidence enough. Everything indicates that you have found it, and then the world wants it—or at least the fruits of it.

There comes another difficult period for you when you really believe that the world has recognized that you have found "the pearl" and that it wants it and you want to pour it out. After you have done this for several years—heartbreaking years—you discover that the world did not want it at all: It merely wanted the fruits which it saw you enjoying. That is why when someone comes to you, claiming that he wants truth, you move very slowly—you are not always sure that he is really sincere. Perhaps he wants only the effects or the results. You soon discover which is which, and what his real purpose is because, if he really wants it, there will be indications that all other things have been thrown aside and by his actions he proves that nothing is as important as truth to him. Then you will not hear, "Well, I can't make it Thursday night, but I'll come Tuesday afternoon. If you can't see me then, I just can't see you!"

When a student really wants the truth, he will come at midnight or at any hour of the day or night, if you but say the word. Do you know that Brown Landone kept office hours all night long? When you made an appointment with him for three o'clock, you had to ask whether it was A.M. or P.M. I have had appointments with him at three o'clock in the morning that lasted until six.

As you become active in this work, you will find that there is no such thing as keeping office hours. A.M. or P.M. means absolutely nothing to you except for keeping the record straight, and the devotion and dedication of those who come to you can in a sense be measured by their concern as to whether their appointment with you is for A.M. or P.M., Thursday or Friday or Sunday; because if they are concerned about such comparative trivialities, then their hearts are not in it—and this path is not meant for those whose hearts and souls and minds are not in God.

If there is an idea in your mind at all that truth is something which can be used, that it is something for personal gain, for personal happiness or personal wealth, do not even begin its study because you will only meet with disappointments and heartaches. There are any number of metaphysical systems that can be used for the purpose of bringing about personal happiness or temporary personal gains. But the Infinite Way cannot be used for such purposes: The Infinite Way can bring only immortality and eternality and all the good that God knows. But that is on an entirely different level than human good, just as spiritual freedom should not be confused with human freedom.

Spiritual freedom, the peace that passes understanding, is not dependent on anything in the outer world. It is dependent on your relationship with the Christ, with God. As that becomes real, as It becomes embodied in you, as It inflames you and that Life becomes your all-in-all, you find yourself living in two worlds, the inner world, the important one, and the outer world, with its share of satisfactions, but not to be taken too seriously and not to be permitted to take up too much time or effort because the eagerness to get back to the Center is so great.

Spiritual Power in World Affairs

As God becomes a reality and we become consciously one with It, It guides every step of our experience; It supplies us; It draws to us all that we need in the world—right friendships, right family relationships, right supply, right activity, right books, right associations, everything that is necessary to advance our cultural and spiritual welfare and provide us with greater opportunity to be of service to the world. I have a deep conviction that for the first time in the history of the entire world spiritual power is going to play a part in human affairs.

Up to this present time, has God really been brought into the human scene, or is there any evidence that God has concerned Itself with human problems? If God had been brought into the human scene, I do not believe that the world would have gone through thousands and thousands of years of wars, tornadoes, earthquakes, famines, and pestilence. Had God been present in human affairs, these things could not have been. Where then has God been during all these years?

The truth is that God is always present in the consciousness of those who are conscious of Its presence. But how many

people have there been who have had this consciousness? The few who lived in monasteries, the few who
lived in ashramas, the few spiritual students of the world,
the few who have tried to found religious organizations
and failed. They knew God and they had the blessing of
God's presence and God's power in their individual
experience.

This blessing, however, did not come down to the
level of the masses. In fact, spiritual truth was never
given to the world at large until the last three-quarters of
a century. Before that time all the religious knowledge of
the world was jealously guarded by the philosophers,
priests, and rabbis. All that the people—the masses—were
ever given were forms, ceremonies, rituals, and creeds.
Did the Hindu masters ever teach those who were below
the level of the spiritual Brahmin? Except for a brief
period in Europe—the period of the Western mystics
during those few centuries from about 1200 to 1700—were
the masses ever taught spiritual truth? How many people
was Jesus able to reach? At the most only a few hundred,
practically nothing as compared with the great numbers
in the world. When has spiritual consciousness ever
reached the level of mass human consciousness?

But a change came about in those years when Christian Science, Unity, and New Thought began to be given
to the world. People were encouraged to meditate,
ponder, read daily spiritual lessons, go to church
Wednesday, go to church Sunday, and then go to church
on other occasions to serve on committees or for daily
noon services. For many years, through Christian
Science, Unity, and New Thought, spiritual truth has
been given to the people, to great numbers of them, to
any who would accept it.

All this has acted like a leaven, so that people who do not even know the meaning of the word, "metaphysics," use the expression, "passing on," instead of dying. Many people who do not know the meaning of metaphysics admit that there is spiritual power or that diseases have been healed and supply has been received through spiritual means. Doctors admit the efficacy of spiritual healing because they have seen case after case healed in the hospitals. As a matter of fact, the psychosomatic medical practitioners have taken a leaf out of the early metaphysical teachings, and some of them now believe in an outmoded form of metaphysics which teaches that there is a mental cause for a physical disease.

The truth is that there is no disease in God's kingdom. You cannot have God *and* a disease, too. There is only one Power, and that is God. Anything else is belief or illusion. In those early days, however, even though the teaching of a mental cause for a physical disease was erroneous, it was a step out of what had gone before. The terminology of religion was used, and God was brought into the healing arts. All this had one important effect: It drove people to the subject of God on some day of the week other than Sunday, and it brought people to the place where they made God a part of their daily experience as a means of overcoming their problems. It does not make any difference how crude the beginning was, it had satisfactory results and good effects. It spread the word to the world that God is not just a Sunday experience, or an experience for the minister alone, the priest or the rabbi, but that God is an experience for you and for me, and that we can reach conscious oneness with God even if we are not ministers, priests, or rabbis.

If you have not been a part of this religious revolution or if you have not at least been a close observer of it, you cannot realize the changes which took place when God was brought into the consciousness of the man in the street. It was probably one of the greatest events that has ever happened in the history of the world. And now for seventy-five years that has been spreading to where even in little metaphysical libraries, truth centers, or Christian Science Reading Rooms, probably two or three hundred people go daily to meditate, to read, and to seek to know more about God. Think of the many homes that are affected by the work that is carried on in the Unity centers, New Thought centers, independent centers, and the Christian Science Churches and Reading Rooms. Try to multiply that around the world.

How can the effect of the million or more copies that have been sold of Ralph Waldo Trine's *In Tune with the Infinite* be measured? Do you know what it could have meant for two million people to have thought about God before this era?

With this much of God in human consciousness—and remember that one grain of God can work miracles—think how this God-consciousness must be leavening thought, influencing our public officials and our international relationships! If it has not as yet had any significant influence, it will have, and in an ever increasing degree. The God-consciousness of this world will some day dominate and control the entire consciousness of the world—political, economic, and social, as well as religious. That will come about because, for the first time, the masses are learning to take God into their experience, not only seven days a week, but they are learning to "pray without ceasing." They are learning to take God into their consciousness even when they sit down for a simple bite of breakfast or lunch.

The thought of the world is being leavened; the thought of the world is being reached with this God-consciousness. It makes no difference which one of the metaphysical movements you name. Each one of them is carrying the word, God, the term, Christ-consciousness, and the idea of God immanent in individual experience to the world. So, each one is acting as a blessing; each one is a light to the world.

The day should come when every metaphysical practitioner should be so thoroughly imbued with the Christ that he can heal, and then whether you go to a New Thought, Unity, Christian Science, or Infinite Way practitioner, you will experience healing.

Let us be honest about this: The teaching itself has nothing to do with the healing. The teaching only serves to open your consciousness to the receptivity of the Christ; and this receptivity to the Christ is what does the healing. All the books—thousands and thousands of them—will not heal a simple headache, even if you could memorize all their contents. The Christ alone is the healer. There is enough truth in the Bible to open consciousness to the Christ, if there were not a single metaphysical book on earth. There is enough truth in any honest metaphysical book to open consciousness to the Christ. As little truth as there is in some of them, there is still enough—enough truth to lead you to the Christ, and that is the leavening influence, not the written word.

Healing will be brought about only as the Christ is introduced into consciousness. You can go to any healer in any of the metaphysical movements and if you find one imbued with the spirit of Truth and the Christ, he will be able to bring forth a healing for you even if he is a part of a movement where the teaching is not on too spiritual a level. The day must come when every practitioner, regardless of his metaphysical background, will be so imbued with the Christ that when a call comes the Christ should answer and bring the healing.

There should be places—and there are some—which would open their doors to people of all churches or no church, to all organizations or no organization, and make it possible for people to meet on the common level of Christhood, not being too concerned with which particular teaching is being followed because over and over again we have been told that "the letter killeth, but the spirit giveth life."[6] I am not too concerned about the books people read, but I am concerned about the people who read them. I am concerned as to whether or not they can find in those books some measure of the Christ, enough to give them the desire to live It and to carry the thought of God out into their human experience.

Remember that it was promised that if there were ten righteous men in the city, the city would be saved. There is a deep spiritual law behind that statement. When there are a few "tens" of righteous people, of God-consciousness people, God-intoxicated people, maybe they will save the town, the nation, or the world. It could well be—it could very, very well be. It may be that the righteous thinking of just a few on the inner plane will touch and reach the consciousness of the world.

We have known of civilizations that have been wiped out, civilizations that were just as far advanced as our own and some that were further advanced. In our complacency, we probably think that we have the greatest degree of civilization attained by man. True, we are perhaps the greatest generation of scientists, mechanical engineers, and "gadgeteers," but we are not the greatest generation of developed civilization. That honor was reserved for other civilizations, and they were wiped out. There was no God who prevented that holocaust either. There never will be until God becomes the level of individual and mass consciousness. Then God will work in our human affairs. You must recognize the validity of this statement because, just as God did not work in your own human affairs to any great extent until you caught some glimpse of the Christ and, from then on, God governed all your human affairs, so God will not work in world affairs until God becomes the real consciousness of thousands and thousands and thousands of people. Then you will find that very God-consciousness influencing material and international affairs.

The Christ-force is so tremendous that when it comes alive, It comes for a universal purpose, not just for the purpose of solving a few of our personal human problems. The Christ is universal good, not personal good. Any truth that is individually true is universally true. Therefore, every time there is an individual demonstration of the Christ-presence, there is a universal demonstration. It only needs to be recognized on a wider scale to be operative in world affairs.

Probably that is why the Bible says that if there be ten righteous men—not just one or two, but ten—if there be ten men with enough spirituality, leavening consciousness, they will influence the others. That does not mean that numbers are required: It means that enough people must be willing to come under the sway of spiritual dominion, because we cannot, with all our spirituality, bring even the members of our own family into heaven, if they do not want to come. It takes a permeating of consciousness, a leavening, so that enough people will really have the desire to give up their dependency on human means.

The Battle Is Not Yours

"Resist not evil." Regardless of the name or nature of your particular problem, stop battling error insofar as you can; try not to fight it too hard. Take the attitude that the battle is not yours; then be still and see the salvation of the Lord. You need not battle: All you have to do is to make the acknowledgment that all that is appearing is for the glory of God. See if you cannot be more relaxed about this healing work and act as if you were really convinced that evil is not a great power.

Suppose right now that you had the personal power to be able to heal a disease. Wouldn't that frighten you? It should! It should! But you do not have such power. The Christ, the Infinite Invisible, is the only healing agency there is in the world. It dispels the illusion of sense, and that is all that is necessary.

The great secret is: "I can of mine own self do nothing[7] . . . I live; yet not I, but Christ liveth in me."[8] The great secret is not how much personal power you can develop as a healer, but how good a vehicle you become for the Christ, how clear a transparency, what degree of Christ-consciousness you develop. In other words, what degree of love of error or hate of error or fear of error is in or out of your consciousness? How much do you really fear error? How much do you really love error? How much do you hate error? That determines how much of a transparency you are for the Christ. It is not how much personal power you have, but how clear you are on the great truth that God is love and that God is no respecter of persons. In Him there is no sin and no disease, and we live and move and have our being in Christ-consciousness.

To all of you who are actively engaged in the healing work, when a call comes, see to what extent you can stop setting up a resistance or denial, rushing in with an, "It isn't true! It isn't true!" See if you can resist doing that and actually believe that it is not true. If you really believe it is not true, you do not have to say it or declare it: You can be content to smile at it because you are able to see through it.

Sometimes you may have to keep this up for a long, long time. The tenacity of error is so strong in some people's thoughts, it is necessary to persist in this practice. We have not yet come to the place where we know with any certainty why one person can be healed in a minute and why it takes two years for another. Perhaps some feel as I do that it has to do with pre-existence; it has to do with the individual's life cycle before he made his appearance on this earth plane. I personally believe that. I believe that since life is eternal, we have always lived, and inasmuch as we have always lived, we must have lived in, or out of, some particular state of consciousness, and therefore some people are very, very much further developed than others.

For example, suppose you, who have reached at least a high enough state of consciousness to be reading and studying truth, were at this moment to pass on. You would not find yourself having to experience all the things you had to go through before you came to this spiritual awareness. You would very likely begin on the next plane where you are at this minute as a spiritually developed Soul—in some cases even much further ahead because often the act of transition is a freeing one.

Our particular concern at this moment, however, is not to speculate as to why one person gets healed quickly and another one does not. Our particular problem is the development of some measure of Christ-consciousness—that divine universal Love, that sense of forgiveness and gratitude—the development of our consciousness to that point where we neither fear, hate, nor love error.

Do not forget that the command of the Master was, "Love thy neighbor."[9] It was not only a command to love God, but to love your neighbor, to love your neighbor as yourself. Sometimes some of us become so absolute about our love for God that we forget our neighbor. But we cannot do that in this work. We want the full measure of the Christ; and therefore, we must not only love God with all our heart and with all our soul, but we must love our neighbor also; and that love must be shown forth in compassion, patience, justice, kindness, forbearance, and joy—a willingness to share all of the good that God has given us.

Above all, we must give up our egotistic belief that we have personal powers as practitioners. Our healings will be in proportion as we realize that all power is given to us through God, through the Christ which strengthens us. And that is the only Source of our power.

This same idea of no personal power is paramount in leading the spiritual or mystical life, in which there is no dependency on person, place, or thing, and no reliance on human contacts—only a dependency and reliance on the inner plane, on our inner contact with God.

If there be any method to demonstration, it is by means of this contact with the Father within. Gain the conscious realization of the presence and power of God within your own being. Regardless of the name or nature of the problem or need, do not try to solve it on the level of the problem. Do not try to solve supply as supply; do not try to solve family relationships as family relationships. Drop all thought of these things. Go within until you actually find that place within your being which gives you the God-response. Then your problems will be solved.

Once you have touched the Christ within your own being, you have touched the wellspring of life more abundant.

Conscious oneness with God! This constitutes conscious oneness with all spiritual being and with every spiritual idea.

Scriptural References & Notes

Chapter 1
1. John 18:36
2. By the author*
3. Psalm 127:1
4. *op. cit.*
5. John 5:30
6. John 14:10
7. Galatians 2:20

Chapter 2
1. John 16:7
2. John 10:27
3. John 10:30
4. John 10:30
5. Luke 15:31
6. Exodus 20:13
7. John 12:32
8. John 5:30
9. John 14:10
10. John 19:11
11. John 14:6
12. John 10:30
13. Psalm 46:10
14. John 8:58
15. Matthew 28:20
16. By the author**

Chapter 3
1. Matthew 6:25
2. Luke 12:30, 32
3. Luke 12:25
4. Isaiah 55:8
5. Jeremiah 31:29
6. John 8:58
7. Matthew 28:20

Chapter 3 (Continued)
8. Zechariah 4:6
9. John 8:58
10. Matthew 28:20
11. John 16:7
12. Galatians 2:20
13. John 18:36
14. Luke 12:22

Chapter 4
1. Luke 15:31
2. By the author*
3. Matthew 16:23

Chapter 5
1. Matthew 5:25
2. John 10:30
3. John 18:36
4. Isaiah 26:3
5. Zechariah4:6
6. Mark 8:18
7. Matthew 6:33
8. Matthew 4:4
9. John 6:31
10. John 6:32, 33, 35

Chapter 6
1. Matthew 7:12
2. John 18:36
3. John 16:33
4. I Corinthians 13:12
5. John 3:2
6. John 14:27
7. Matthew 26:40
8. John 16:7

Chapter 7
1. John 10:30
2. Luke 15:31
3. Matthew 6:25
4. Psalm 23:2
5. John 16:33
6. Matthew 11:3
7. Matthew 11:4, 5

Chapter 8
1. Matthew 7:12
2. Matthew 25:36
3. Matthew 6:27
4. Matthew 5:36
5. Luke 12:22
6. Luke 5:23
7. Mark 2:9
8. I Samuel 3:9
9. Psalm 46:10
10. John 5:30, 31
11. John 7:16

Chapter 9
1. John 5:30
2. John 14:10
3. Isaiah 26:3
4. By the author.*

Chapter 10
1. John 18:36
2. Matthew 6:33
3. Matthew 4:4
4. Matthew 22:21
5. John 4:32
6. John 10:27
7. John 4:32
8. John 16:33

Chapter 10 (Continued)
9. John 12:32
10. John 4:32

Chapter 11
1. John 8:58
2. John 8:58
3. Matthew 28:20
4. Matthew 4:4
5. Matthew 5:25
6. Matthew 12:13
7. Matthew 9:5
8. John 19:11

Chapter 12
1. I Samuel 3:9
2. Psalm 46:10
3. John 10:30
4. Isaiah 26:3
5. John 18:36
6. John 15:16

Chapter 13
1. John 10:10
2. Matthew 6:33
3. John 18:36
4. John 16:33
5. Matthew 7:14
6. II Corinthians 3:6
7. John 5:30
8. Galatians 2:20
9. Matthew 22:39

* *The Infinite Way,* (c) 1947, 1956, reprinted 1997 by Acropolis Books, Inc.

** *Spiritual Interpretation of Scripture,* © 1947 Joel S. Goldsmith (Marina del Ray, CA, DeVorss & Company)